Nicky Epstein's

Knitted Embellishments

350 Appliqués
Borders
Cords and more!

INTERWEAVE PRESS

To my husband, Howard, who has spent many hours reading stitch patterns and charts to me so I could meet deadlines (even when the Giants were playing).

Interior Design, Dean Howes
Cover Design, Elizabeth R. Mrofka
Illustration, Gayle Ford
Technical Editing, Dorothy T. Ratigan
Photography, Joe Coca

Text copyright 1999, Nicky Epstein

 Interweave Press, Inc.
201 East Fourth Street
Loveland, Colorado 80537

Library of Congress Cataloging-in-Publication Data

Epstein, Nicky.
    Nicky Epstein's knitted embellishments: 350 appliqués, borders, cords
and more!/by Nicky Epstein.
        p.   cm.
    Includes index.
    ISBN 1–883010–39–X
    1. Knitting—Patterns. 2. Fancy work. 3. Clothing and dress.
4. House furnishings. I. Title. II. Title: Knitted
embellishments.
TT825.E6423   1999
746.43'2041—dc21   98–32299
                                                              CIP

First Printing: 10M:299:RRD

Acknowledgements

I want to thank many people, friends both professional and personal, who have encouraged me over the years and helped me widen my horizons: editors such as Eleanor Bernat, B. J. Berti, Lola Erhlich, Pat Harste, and Nora O'Leary, who taught me not to compromise my talent or integrity; the many wonderful knitters who have always come through on deadlines when I needed extra hands; all my students and readers who actually knit my designs; and my steadfast friends, Emily and Ann Brenner, Mary Hustead, Chris Kitch, Mary K. Spagnuolo, and Diane Weitzul, who are always only a phone call away.

Thanks also go to Vincent Caputo, Shelley Charney, Eileen Curry, Sonja Dagress, and Dorothy Ratigan for the many hours they spent knitting, technical editing, and proofreading.

Special thanks go to my husband, Howard, for his unbiased honesty and biased support throughout this project, and to my mother, Carmella, and grandmother, Anna, who are always in my heart.

Finally, I'm grateful to the entire staff at Interweave Press, particularly Ann Budd, Gayle Ford, and Judith Durant, for making this labor-intensive work come together so beautifully and professionally.

Happy Knitted Embellishments!

—Nicky Epstein

Table of Contents

The Heart of the Matter

In my many years of designing for knitting magazines and national publications such as *Vogue Knitting, Woman's Day, Family Circle, Knitter's,* and *Interweave Knits,* and for yarn companies such as Rowan, Tahki, and Reynolds, I've found that an editor is more likely to buy designs that include some special detail. For me, these extra touches are usually unique borders, edges, or embellishments.

Some of the examples in this book are traditional patterns gleaned from many sources. I have added variations to some of these time-honored patterns and presented them along with my original patterns and techniques.

This book is intended to encourage all knitters, from beginners to experts, to expand their creative horizons with these versatile and unusual knitted design techniques. I put these ideas forth and encourage you to adapt and expand on them to suit your own needs. When judicially applied, these techniques bring new creativity to a knitter's design and take the piece beyond the ordinary. The best results happen when technique and imagination are in concert, so don't be afraid to experiment.

You will find sketches throughout this book that demonstrate how borders, edges, and embellishment can enhance a piece. Here, I've rendered a simple heart design in some of the techniques we'll explore. With these techniques and your own imagination, there's no limit to what you'll be able to create.

Allover Pattern

(multiple of 14 sts + 4)

Row 1: (RS) Purl.
Row 2: *K8, p2, k4; rep from *, end last rep k8.
Row 3: P4, *p3, 1/1RC, 1/1LC, p7; rep from *.
Row 4: *K7, p4, k3; rep from *, end last rep k7.
Row 5: P4, *p2, 1/1RC, k2, 1/1LC, p6; rep from *.
Row 6: *K6, p6, k2; rep from *, end last rep k6.
Row 7: P4, *p1, 1/1RC, k4, 1/1LC, p5; rep from *.
Row 8: *K5, p8, k1; rep from *, end last rep k5.
Row 9: P4, *1/1RC, k6, 1/1LC, p4; rep from *.
Row 10: *K4, p10; rep from *, k4.
Row 11: P4, *k3, 1/1RC, 1/1LC, k3, p4; rep from *.

Row 12: *K4, p4, k2, p4; rep from *, k4.

Row 13: P4, *1/1LC, 1/1RC, p2, 1/1LC, 1/1RC, p4; rep from *.

Row 14: *K5, p2, k4, p2, k1; rep from *, end last rep k5.

Row 15: P4, *p1, M1, ssk, p4, k2tog, M1, p5; rep from *.

Rows 16 and 18: Knit.

Row 17: Purl.

Rep Rows 1–18 for desired length.

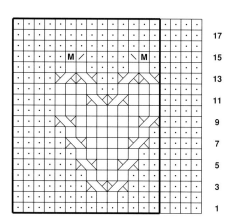

Vertical Panel

(panel of 10 sts; sample bordered with rev St st)

Row 1: (RS) Knit.

Row 2 and all even-numbered rows: Purl.

Rows 3 and 11: K3, 1/1RC, 1/1LC, k3.

Row 5: K2, 1/1RC, k2, 1/1LC, k2.

Row 7: K1, 1/1RC, k4, 1/1LC, k1.

Row 9: 1/1RC, k6, 1/1LC.

Row 13: 1/1LC, 1/1RC, k2, 1/1LC, 1/1RC.

Row 15: K1, M1, ssk, k4, k2tog, M1, k1.

Row 16: Purl.

Rep Rows 1–16 for desired length.

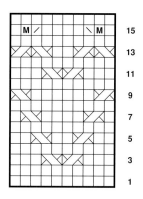

Lace

(cast on multiple of 12 sts + 3)

Row 1: (RS) K2, *yo, k2tog, k3, yo, k1, yo, k3, ssk, yo, k1; rep from *, end last rep k2—mult of 14 sts + 3.

Row 2 and all even-numbered rows: Purl.

Row 3: K2, *k1, yo, k4tog, yo, k3, yo, sl next 4 sts individually kwise, insert left needle into fronts of these sts and knit them tog tbl, yo, k2; rep from *, end last rep k3—mult of 12 sts + 3.

Row 5: K2, *k1, k2tog, yo, k5, yo, ssk, k2; rep from *, end last rep k3.

Row 7: K2, *k2tog, yo, k7, yo, ssk, k1; rep from *, end last rep k2.

Row 9: K1, k2tog, *yo, k9, yo, sl 2tog kwise, k1, p2sso; rep from *, end last rep ssk, k1.

Rep Rows 1–10 for desired length.

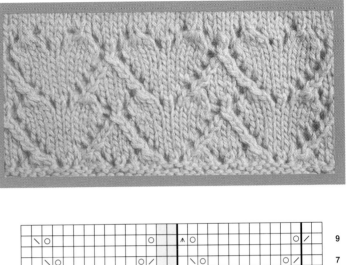

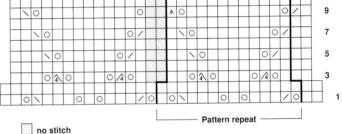

☐ no stitch

Pattern repeat

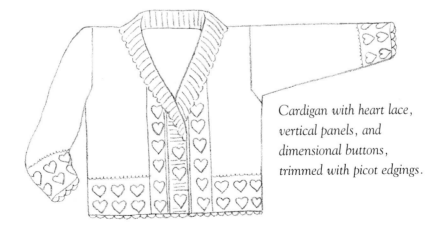

Cardigan with heart lace, vertical panels, and dimensional buttons, trimmed with picot edgings.

Intarsia

(worked over 19 sts and 21 rows)

With the contrast yarn wound on a bobbin, work as charted.

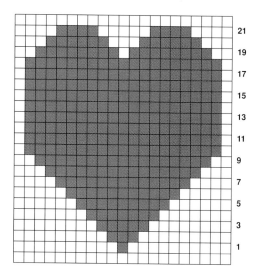

Duplicate Stitch

(worked over 9 sts and 11 rows)

Work duplicate stitch (page 189) according to the chart.

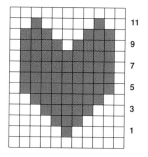

Cross-Stitch

(worked over 9 sts and 11 rows)

Following Duplicate-stitch chart (page 10), embroider a cross-stitch (page 190) on top of each knitted stitch.

Embossed Stitch

(worked over 17 sts and 30 rows)

Following chart, work heart motif in St st (shaded) and background in garter st.

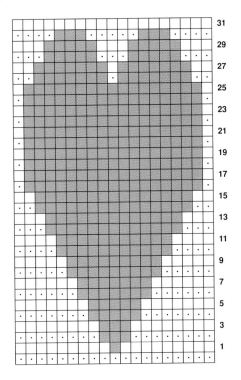

Fair Isle

(multiple of 10 sts)

Working in the Fair Isle technique, follow chart.

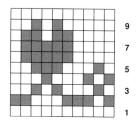

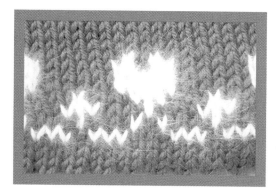

Embroidery

Work chain sts (page 196) and duplicate st (page 189) to form hearts.

Appliqué Heart

Top of heart: CO 3 sts. With separate ball of yarn, CO 3 more sts on same needle—6 sts total.

Row 1: (RS) *[K1, M1] 2 times, k1; rep from * on second set of sts—5 sts each set.

Row 2 and all even-numbered rows: Purl.

Row 3: *K1, M1, knit to last st, M1, k1; rep from * over second set of sts—7 sts each set.

Rows 5 and 7: Rep Row 3—11 sts each set after Row 7.

Heart body:

Row 9: Join sets as follows: K1, M1, k9, k2tog, k9, M1, k1—23 sts. Cut second yarn.

Row 11: Knit.

Row 13 and all odd-numbered rows through 29: K1, ssk, knit to last 3 sts, k2tog, k1—2 sts dec'd each row; 5 sts rem after Row 29.

Row 31: K1, sl 1, k2tog, psso, k1—3 sts.

Row 33: Sl 1, k2tog, psso—1 st. Fasten off.

Appliqué with Ruffle

Work Appliqué heart as above.

Ruffle: (cast on multiple of 2 sts + 1)

Row 1: K1, *p1, M1, k1; rep from *.

Row 2 and all even-numbered rows: Knit the knits and purl the purls.

Row 3: K1, *p2, M1, k1; rep from *.

Row 5: K1, *p3, M1, k1; rep from *.

Row 7: K1, *p4, M1, k1; rep from *.

Row 9: K1, *p5, M1, k1; rep from *.

BO all sts in knit.

Note: If you prefer to knit in the round, pick up and knit sts around the edge of the heart and work the ruffle directly on the heart.

Color Pattern

(worked over 13 sts and 13 rows, excluding border)

Working in the Fair Isle technique, follow chart.

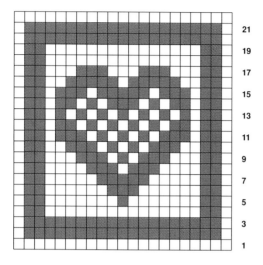

Bobble

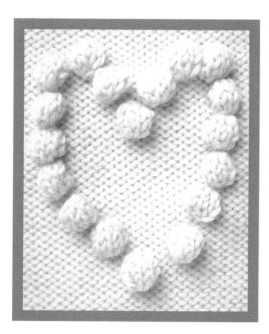

Bobble: CO 1 st. ([K1f&b] 2 times, k1) in same st—5 sts. [Knit 1 row, purl 1 row] 2 times. On next row, k2tog, k1, k2tog—3 sts. On next row, sl 1, p2tog, psso—1 st. Fasten off.

Make 18 bobbles, leaving long tails for CO and BO. Attach bobbles to background in heart shape by inserting the CO and BO tails through the background and tying them together.

Knit Cord

(worked on seed st background)

Knit cord: CO 5 sts onto a double-pointed needle. *K5, do not turn work. Slide sts to right end of needle. Pull yarn around back of sts to tighten. Rep from * for desired length. BO all sts or leave on needle for grafting.

Work knit cord for desired length. Pin cord into a heart shape (beg at the point of the heart) onto background. With RS facing, sew cord in place. Use the Kitchener st (page 261) to graft the ends tog.

Mock Cable Knit Cord

(worked on rev St st background)

Make two 4-st knit cords as described above for desired length. Attach cords to background forming heart shapes separated by mock cables, worked by twisting the two cords together 3 times.

Faux Button

(Faux button is used with snap closure)

Top of heart: (Make 2) CO 3 sts. With separate ball of yarn, CO 3 more sts onto same needle.

Rows 1 and 3: (RS) ([K1, M1] 2 times, k1) on each set of sts— 5 sts each set.

Row 2 and all even-numbered rows: Purl.

Row 3: K1, M1, k3, M1, k1—7 sts each set.

Heart Body:

Row 5: Working with one yarn only, join sets as follows: k7, M1, k7—15 sts total.

Row 7: Knit.

Rows 9, 11, 13, 15, 17, and 19: Ssk, knit to last 2 sts, k2tog—2 sts dec'd each row—3 sts after Row 19.

Row 21: Sl 1, k2tog, psso. Fasten off.

   With WS facing, sew the 2 heart pieces tog, leaving a small opening. Stuff with fiberfill. Sew rem seam.

Dimensional Ornament

Top of heart: (Make 2) CO 3 sts. With separate ball of yarn, CO 3 more sts on same needle—6 sts total.

Row 1: (RS) *[K1, M1] 2 times, k1; rep from * on second set of sts—5 sts each set.

Row 2 and all even-numbered rows: Purl.

Row 3: *K1, M1, k3, M1, k1; rep from * on second set of sts—7 sts each set.

Row 5: *K1, M1, k5, M1, k1; rep from * on second set of sts—9 sts each set; 18 sts total.

Heart body:

Row 7: Join sets as follows: K1, M1, k7, k2tog, k7, M1, k1—19 sts. Cut second yarn.

Row 9: Knit.

Rows 11, 13, 15, 17, 19, 21, and 23: K1, ssk, knit to last 3 sts, k2tog, k1—2 sts dec'd each row; 5 sts rem after Row 23.

Row 25: K1, sl 1, k2tog, psso, k1—3 sts.

Row 27: Sl 1, k2tog, psso—1 st. Fasten off.

   With WS facing, sew the 2 heart pieces tog, leaving a small opening. Stuff with fiberfill. Sew rem seam.

Appliqué

Appliqué knitting is a versatile technique in which motifs are knitted separately and then sewn onto a background. They can be sewn on singly or in groups for quick and impressive results. I draw much of my inspiration from appliqué quilting, and have included many popular quilting motifs such as trees, leaves, flowers, fruits, vegetables, hearts, and bows. The dimensions and textures of the motifs give a knitted piece a look unlike that of any other knitting technique. Plain sweaters and afghans (even those made on a knitting machine) can be transformed into artistic statements with the addition of hand-knitted appliqués.

Flowers

Crocheted flowers are commonly used to embellish knitted backgrounds, but I hope the following examples will inspire you to knit them instead. They're quick and easy, so you can be creative. Experiment with different textures and colors. When knitted with fine beautiful yarns, flowers can be frail and lovely. When knitted with bright novelty yarn, they can be bold and vibrant. Beautiful flowers can be created with basic stitch patterns; add color and the varieties are endless.

The following samples include many yarn types—angora, cotton, chenille, silk, wool, metallic, and rayon. Beads, bobbles, and embroidery are used for some of the centers. Refer to the section on knitted leaves (pages 35–56) for foliage to enhance the flowers. Apply the flowers alone or in bouquets, with leaves, stems, and embroidery embellishment.

Morning Glory

(multiple of 9 sts + 4; sample worked on 58 sts)

Beg with a dark color (A), change to a light color (B) on Row 6, and change to a center color (C) on Row 10. Leave an 8" (20.5- cm) tail at color changes for seaming.

Rows 1, 3, 5, and 7: (WS) Purl.

Rows 2 and 6: (RS) K3, *yo, k2, ssk, k2tog, k2, yo, k1; rep from *, end last rep k2.

Row 4: K2, *yo, k2, ssk, k2tog, k2, yo, k1; rep from *, end last rep k3.

Row 8: *K1, k3tog; rep from *, end k2—30 sts.

Row 9: *P1, p3tog; rep from *, end p2—16 sts.
Row 10: *K2tog; rep from *—8 sts.

Cut yarn leaving 12" (30.5-cm) tail. With tapestry needle, thread tail through rem sts on needle. Gather up and fasten securely. Sew seam. Work straight sts (page 192) and French knot (page 203) in center.

Basic Flower

(multiple of 9 sts + 1; sample worked on 55 sts)

Rows 1, 3, 5, and 7: (WS) Purl.
Row 2: K1, *yo, k2, ssk, k2tog, k2, yo, k1; rep from *.
Rows 4 and 6: *K2, ssk, k2tog, k2, yo, k1, yo; rep from *, end last rep k1.
Row 8: K1, k2tog, *k1, ssk, k2tog; rep from *, end k2—34 sts.
Row 9: P2, *p3tog, p1; rep from *—18 sts.
Row 10: *K2tog; rep from *—9 sts.

Cut yarn leaving 12" (30.5-cm) tail. With tapestry needle, thread tail through rem sts on needle. Gather up and fasten securely. Sew seam. Work French knot (page 203) in center.

Small Flower

(multiple of 9 sts + 4; sample worked on 58 sts)

Rows 1, 3, and 5: (WS) Purl.
Row 2: K3, *yo, k2, ssk, k2tog, k2, yo, k1; rep from *, end last rep k2.
Row 4: K2, *yo, k2, ssk, k2tog, k2, yo, k1; rep from *, end last rep k3.
Row 6: *K1, k3tog; rep from *, end k2—30 sts.
Row 7: *P1, p3tog; rep from *, end p2—16 sts.
Row 8: With CC, *k2tog; rep from *—8 sts.

Cut yarn leaving 8" (20.5 cm) tail. With tapestry needle, thread tail through rem sts on needle. Gather up and fasten securely. Sew seam. Work French knot (page 203) in center.

Note: The following six flowers are based on the same basic ruffle stitch.

Large Ruffle Flower

(odd number of sts; sample worked on 27 sts)

CO 27 sts, leaving a long tail for seaming.
Row 1: (RS) K1, *p1, k1; rep from *.
Rows 2, 4, 6, 8, and 10: Knit the knits and purl the purls.
Row 3: K1, *p1, M1 pwise, k1; rep from *—40 sts.
Row 5: K1, *p2, M1 pwise, k1; rep from *—53 sts.
Row 7: K1, *p3, M1 pwise, k1; rep from *—66 sts.
Row 9: K1, *p4, M1 pwise, k1; rep from *—79 sts.
    BO all sts. With tapestry needle, thread CO tail
through CO sts, gather, and pull tightly. Sew seam. Sew beads to center. Add leaves, if desired.

Ruffle Rose

(odd number of sts; sample worked on 37 sts)

CO 37 sts, leaving a long tail for seaming.
Row 1: K1, *p1, k1; rep from *.
Rows 2, 4, 6, 8, and 10: Knit the knits and purl the purls.
Row 3: K1, *p1, M1 pwise, k1; rep from *—55 sts.
Row 5: K1, *p2, M1 pwise, k1; rep from *—73 sts.
Row 7: K1, *p3, M1 pwise, k1; rep from *—91 sts.
Row 9: K1, *p4, M1 pwise, k1; rep from *—109 sts.
    BO all sts. Roll the ruffle edge and seam the CO edge to form a rose shape. Add leaves, if desired.
Felted (page 263), the ruffle rose is perfect for trimming a hat.

Large Ruffle Flower with Bobbles

Bobble (MB): ([K1, yo] 2 times, then k1) in same st—5 sts. Turn. K5,
    turn, p5, pass 2nd, 3rd, 4th, and 5th st over 1st st.

CO 27 sts, leaving a long tail for seaming. Work rows 1–10 of Large Ruffle Flower (above)—79 sts.
Next row: K1, *p5, MB; rep form *, end MB. BO all sts. Fasten off.
    With tapestry needle, thread CO tail through CO sts, gather, and pull
tightly. Sew seam. CO 1 st and make separate bobble for center.

Medium Ruffle Flower with Picot

(odd number of sts; sample worked on 19 sts)

CO 19 sts, leaving a long tail for seaming.
Row 1: (RS) K1, *p1, k1; rep from *.
Rows 2, 4, 6, 8, 10, and 12: Knit the knits and purl the purls.
Row 3: K1, *p1, M1 pwise, k1; rep from *—28 sts.
Row 5: K1, *p2, M1 pwise, k1; rep from *—37 sts.
Row 7: K1, *p3, M1 pwise, k1; rep from *—46 sts.
Row 9: K1, *p4, M1 pwise, k1; rep from *—55 sts.
Row 11: K1, *p5, M1 pwise, k1; rep from *—64 sts.

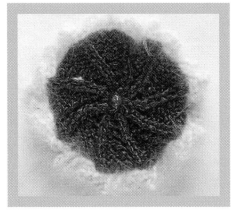

   Work picot on RS (shown in CC) as follows: BO 2 sts, *sl rem
st on right needle onto left needle, CO 2 sts, BO 4 sts; rep from *, end last rep BO 2. Fasten off. Thread CO
tail through CO sts, gather, and pull tightly. Sew seam. Sew bead or work a French knot (page 203) to center.

Double Ruffle Flower

Bobble: CO 1 st. ([K1, yo] 2 times, then k1) in same st—5 sts.
   Turn. K5, turn, p5, pass 2nd, 3rd, 4th, and 5th st over 1st st.

   Work through Row 10 of Medium Ruffle Flower (above), then
work picot edge. With new yarn, work through Row 8 of same
flower, then work picot edge. Place the smaller flower on top of
larger flower and sew tog. Knit a single bobble and attach to flower
center. Add leaves, if desired.

Moon Flower

(odd number of sts; sample worked on 15 sts)

CO 15 sts, leaving a long tail for seaming.
Row 1: (RS) K1, *p1, k1; rep from *.
Rows 2, 4, 6, 8, 10, and 12: Knit the knits and purl the purls.
Row 3: K1, *p1, M1 pwise, k1; rep from *—22 sts.
Row 5: K1, *p2, M1 pwise, k1; rep from *—29 sts.
Row 7: K1, *p3, M1 pwise, k1; rep from *—36 sts.
Row 9: K1, *p4, M1 pwise, k1; rep from *—43 sts.
Row 11: K1, *p5, M1 pwise, k1; rep from *—50 sts.

Work 4 rows rev St st. BO all sts. Thread CO tail through CO sts, gather, and pull tightly. Sew seam. Sew 1 bead to the center and on each spoke of the flower, and add a beaded ribbon to the edge.

Five-Point Pinwheel Flower

Point: CO 2 sts. Inc 1 st at beg of each row until there are 11 sts. Break yarn. Make 4 more points, casting on sts for each point onto an empty needle and breaking yarn on all but the last point.

Knit across all 5 points—55 sts. Knit 2 rows.
Next row: K2tog across, end k1—28 sts.
Next row: K2tog across—14 sts.
Next row: K2tog across—7 sts.
   Pass 6 sts over first st—1 st. Fasten off. Sew seam. Sew beads to flower center.

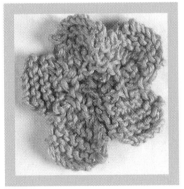

Five-Scallop Garter-Stitch Flower

Scallop: CO 5 sts. Inc 1 st at beg of each row until there are 9 sts. Break yarn. Make 4 more scallops the same way, casting on each scallop on an empty needle and breaking yarn on all but the last scallop.

Knit across all 5 scallops—45 sts.
Next row: *K2tog; rep from *, end k1—23 sts.
Next row: *K2tog; rep from *, end k1—12 sts.
Next row: *K2tog; rep from *—6 sts.
   Gather rem sts tog and fasten off. Sew seam. Sew beads to flower center.

Garter-Stitch Double Flower

   Make, then place one Five-Scallop Garter-Stitch Flower (above) in the center of a Five-Point Pinwheel Flower (above). Sew beads to flower center.

Large Star Flower

(multiple of 10 sts + 2; sample worked on 52 sts)

Bobble: CO 1 st. ([K1, yo] 2 times, then k1) in same st—5 sts. Turn. [K5, turn, p5, turn] 2 times, pass 2nd, 3rd, 4th, and 5th st over 1st st.

Row 1: (WS) K1, *M1, k1, M1, k3, sl 2tog kwise, k1, p2sso, k3; rep from *, end last rep k4.

Row 2: K1, *k3, sl 1 wyf, k6; rep from *, end last rep k7.

Row 3: K2, *M1, k1, M1, k3, sl 2tog kwise, k1, p2sso, k3; rep from *.

Row 4: *K3, sl 1 wyf, k6; rep from *, end last rep k8.

Row 5: *K3, M1, k1, M1, k3, sl 2tog kwise, k1, p2sso; rep from *, end k2.

Row 6: K2, *sl 1 wyf, k9; rep from *.

Row 7: K4, *M1, k1, M1, k3, sl 2tog kwise, k1, p2sso, k3; rep from *, end last rep k1.

Row 8: K1, *sl 1 wyf, k9; rep from *, end last rep k10.

Row 9: K4, *sl 2tog kwise, k1, p2sso, k2; rep from *, end sl 2tog kwise, k1, p2sso—32 sts.

Row 10: *K2tog; rep from *—16 sts.

Row 11: *K2tog; rep from *—8 sts.

Cut yarn leaving 8" (20.5-cm) tail. With tapestry needle, thread tail through rem sts on needle. Gather up and fasten securely. Sew seam. Make bobble and sew to center.

Small Star Flower

(multiple of 10 sts; sample worked on 50 sts)

Row 1: (WS) *K4, sl 2 sts (1 at a time) kwise, k1, p2sso, k3; rep from *— 40 sts.

Row 2: K3, *sl 1 wyf, k7; rep from *, end last rep k4.

Row 3: K3, *sl 2tog kwise, k1, p2sso, k5; rep from *, end last rep k2— 30 sts.

Row 4: K2, *sl 1 wyf, k5; rep from *, end last rep k3.

Row 5: K2, *sl 2tog kwise, k1, p2sso, k3; rep from *, end last rep k1—20 sts.

Row 6: K1, *sl 1 wyf, k3; rep from *, end last rep k2.

Row 7: K1, *sl 2tog kwise, k1, p2sso, k1; rep from *, end last rep sl 2tog kwise—10 sts.

Row 8: *Sl 1 wyf, k1; rep from *.

Row 9: *K2tog; rep from *—5 sts.

Cut yarn leaving 8" (20.5 cm) tail. With tapestry needle, thread tail through rem sts on needle. Gather up and fasten securely. Sew seam. Sew beads to center.

Double Star Flower

Make one Large and one Small Star Flower (page 22). Place small flower in center of large flower and stitch together in center. Sew beads to center and each point. Add leaves, if desired

Note: The following five flowers are based on the same basic scallop stitch.

Basic Five-Petal Blossom

(multiple of 11 sts + 2; sample worked on 57 sts)

Row 1: (WS) Purl.

Row 2: K2, *k1, sl this st back to left needle, lift the next 8 sts on left needle over this st and off needle, [yo] 2 times, knit the 1st st again, k2; rep from *—27 sts.

Row 3: P1, *p2tog, drop 1 yo loop, ([k1f&b] 2 times) in rem yo of previous row, p1; rep from * to last st, p1—32 sts.

Row 4: (shown in CC) K1, *k3tog; rep from *, end k1—12 sts.

Row 5: *P2tog; rep from *—6 sts. Sl 2nd, 3rd, 4th, 5th, and 6th st over 1st st. Fasten off.

Sew seam. Work French knot (page 203) in center.

Petite Fleur

(multiple of 11 sts + 2; sample worked on 68 sts)

Row 1: (RS) Purl.

Row 2: K2, *k1, slip this st back to left needle, lift the next 8 sts on left needle over this st and off needle, [yo] 2 times, knit the 1st st again, k2; rep from *.

Row 3: K1, *p2tog, drop 1 yo loop, ([k1f&b] 2 times) in rem yo of previous row, p1; rep from * to last st, k1.

Rows 4, 5, and 6: Knit.

Row 7: (shown in CC) K1, *k2tog; rep from * to last st, k1—17 sts.

Row 8: K1, *k2tog; rep from *—9 sts.

    Cut yarn leaving 12" (30.5-cm) tail. With tapestry needle, thread tail through rem sts on needle. Gather up and fasten securely. Add leaves, if desired.

1x1 Rib Scallop Flower

(mult of 11 sts + 2; sample worked on 68 sts)

Row 1: (RS) Purl.

Row 2: K2, *k1, slip this st back to left needle, lift the next 8 sts on left needle over this st and off needle, [yo] 2 times, knit the 1st st again, k2; rep from *.

Row 3: K1, *p2tog, drop 1 yo, ([k1f&b] 2 times) in rem yo, p1; rep from * to last st, k1.

Rows 4–8: *P1, k1; rep from *.

Row 9: *K2tog; rep from *—19 sts.

Row 10: P1 *p2tog; rep from *—10 sts.

    Cut yarn leaving 12" (30.5-cm) tail. With tapestry needle, thread tail through rem sts on needle. Gather up and fasten securely. Sew seam. Sew beads to center. Add leaves, if desired.

Canterbury Bell

CO 57 sts.

Row 1: (RS) Purl.

Row 2: K2, *k1, slip this st back to left needle, lift the next 8 sts on left needle over this st and off needle, [yo] 2 times, knit the first st again, k2; rep from *.

Row 3: P1, *p2tog, drop 1 yo, ([k1f&b] 2 times) in rem yo, p1; rep from *, end last rep p2—32 sts.

Rows 4–8: *K2, p2; rep from *.

Row 9: *K2tog, p2tog; rep from *—16 sts.

Rows 10–12: *K1, p1; rep from *.

Row 13: *K2tog; rep from *—8 sts.

Row 14: *P2tog; rep from *—4 sts.

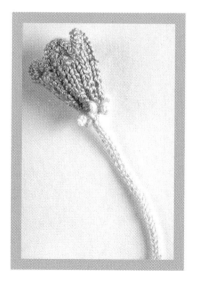

With dpns, work knit cord (page 149) for desired length (shown in CC). Make Picot Chain Flower (page 32) and attach to base of cord for leaves. Sew seam. Stuff fiberfill or cotton ball in bell for shaping.

Pansy

(multiple of 12 sts + 2)

Flower back: With A, CO 26 sts.

Row 1: (RS) Purl.

Row 2: K2, *k1, slip this st back to left needle, lift the next 8 sts on left needle over this st and off needle, [yo] 2 times, knit the first st again, k2; rep from *.

Row 3: K1, *p2tog, drop 1 yo, ([k1f&b] 2 times) in rem yo, p1; rep from * to last st, k1—14 sts.

Row 4: *K3tog; rep from *, end k2tog—5 sts.

Row 5: P2tog, p1, p2tog—3 sts.

BO all sts.

Flower front: With B, CO 38 sts.

Row 1: (RS) Purl.

Row 2: K2, *k1, slip this st back to left needle, lift the next 9 sts on left needle over this st and off needle, [yo] 2 times, knit the first st again, k2; rep from *.

Row 3: K1, *p2tog, drop 1 yo, ([k1f&b] 2 times) in rem yo, p1; rep from * to last st, k1—20 sts.

Row 4: Change to A. *K3tog; rep from *, end k2—8 sts.

Row 5: Purl.

BO all sts. Sew flower front to flower back. Embroider 3 straight sts (page 192) on each front petal. Work French knot (page 203) in center, wrapping yarn 5 times around needle.

Picot Flower with Beads

Using provisional method (page 259), CO 61 sts.

Rows 1, 3, 5, and 7: (RS) Knit.

Rows 2 and 6: Purl.

Row 4: P1, *yo, p2tog; rep from *.

Row 8: Carefully remove waste yarn from CO sts and place live sts on a spare dpn. Hold this needle in front of and parallel to working needle. Fold at picot edge. *P2tog (1 st from each needle); rep from *.

25

Row 9: K4, *sl 2tog kwise, k1, p2sso, k3, sl 1 wyib, k3; rep from *, end sl 2tog kwise, k1, p2sso, k4—49 sts.

Row 10 and all even-numbered rows: Purl.

Row 11: K3, *sl 2tog kwise, k1, p2sso, k2, sl 1 wyib, k2; rep from *, end sl 2tog kwise, k1, p2sso, k3—37 sts.

Row 13: K2, *sl 2tog kwise, k1, p2sso, k1, sl 1 wyib, k1; rep from *, end sl 2tog kwise, k1, p2sso, k2—25 sts.

Row 15: K1, *sl 2tog kwise, k1, p2sso, sl 1 wyib; rep from *, end sl 2tog kwise, k1, p2sso, k1—25 sts.

Row 17: K1, *sl 2tog kwise, k1, p2sso; rep from *, end k1—13 sts.

Row 19: K1, *k2tog; rep from *—7 sts.

   Cut yarn leaving 12" (30.5-cm) tail. With tapestry needle, thread tail through rem sts on needle. Gather up and fasten securely. Sew seam. Sew beads to center and between each spoke. Add leaves, if desired.

Flora Bunda

CO 10 sts.

Rows 1, 2, 5, and 6: Knit.

Rows 3 and 7: BO 7 sts, knit to end—3 sts.

Row 4: K3, turn work, using the knitted method (page 259), CO 7 sts.

Rep Rows 4–7 28 more times or for desired length. BO all sts on Row 7.

   Form into a stacked circle and sew in place. Work French knot (page 203) in center, wrapping yarn around needle 5 times.

Arctic Queen

CO 5 sts. *BO 4 sts; using the knitted method (page 259), CO 4 sts; rep from * for desired length, end BO 4 sts. Change to CC. Knit CO 3 sts, BO 3 sts; rep from * 5 times. BO rem st. Beg with CC for the center, wind knitted length in a spiral to form flower. Sew in place. With stem color, *knit CO 9 sts, BO 8 sts; rep from * once. Sew in place. Note: To make a larger flower, CO more sts (always binding off 1 less st than CO) and work more petals.

Mumzy

Note: Sample worked with double strand of ribbon yarn.

CO 41 sts.

Row 1: (WS) K1, *make loop (see below), k1; rep from *.

Row 2: Knit.

Row 3: K2, *make loop, k1; rep from *, end k2.

Row 4: K2 *k2tog; rep from *, end k1—31 sts

Row 5: K1, *make loop, k1; rep from *.

Row 6: *K1, k2tog; rep from *, end k2—17 sts.

Row 7: K1, *make loop, k1; rep from *.

Row 8: K1, *k2tog; rep from *, end k2—10 sts.

Row 9: [K2tog] 5 times—5 sts.

Cut yarn leaving 12" (30.5-cm) tail. With tapestry needle, thread tail through rem sts on needle. Gather up and fasten securely. Sew seam. Sew beads to center.

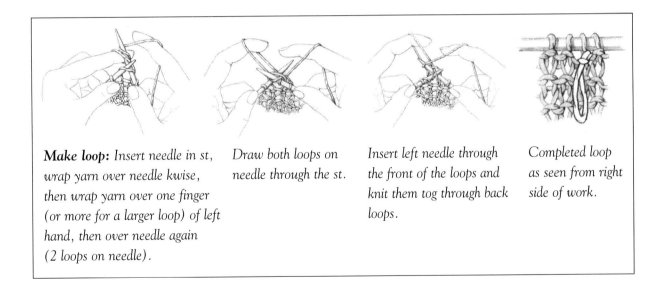

Make loop: *Insert needle in st, wrap yarn over needle kwise, then wrap yarn over one finger (or more for a larger loop) of left hand, then over needle again (2 loops on needle).*

Draw both loops on needle through the st.

Insert left needle through the front of the loops and knit them tog through back loops.

Completed loop as seen from right side of work.

Gossamer Flower with Spiral Beaded Center
(multiple of 3 sts + 1)

CO 52 sts.

Rows 1, 3, 5, 7, and 9: K1b, *p2, k1b; rep from *.

Rows 2, 4, 6, 8, and 10: P1, *k1b, k1, p1; rep from *.

Row 11: K1b, *sl next st off needle and allow it to drop to CO edge, p1, k1b; rep from *—35 sts.

Row 12: P1, *k1b, p1; rep from *.

Row 13: K1, *k2tog; rep from *—18 sts.

Row 14: *P2tog; rep from *—9 sts.

   Pass last 8 sts over first st—1 st. Fasten off. Sew seam. String beads on thread and sew to center forming a spiral.

Gossamer Rose

CO 106 sts. Work Rows 1–14 of Gossamer Flower (above). K2tog and BO at the same time. Roll and stitch at BO edge, beg at center.

Basic Petal I

Individual petals are worked from CO edge (center of flower) to outer edge. To join the petals together, run a threaded needle through their CO edges and gather all sts tog. Fasten off.

Poppy

Large Petal: (Make 5) CO 3 sts.

Rows 1 and 7: Knit.

Rows 2, 4, 6, 8, 10, 12, and 14: Purl.

Row 3: *K1, CO 1; rep from * to last st, k1—5 sts.

Row 5 : Rep Row 3—9sts.

Row 9: *K1, CO 1; rep from * to last st, k1—17 sts.

Rows 11 and 13: *Ssk, knit to last 2 sts, k2tog—13 sts after Row 13.

Row 15: Ssk, BO to last 2 sts, k2tog, and pass last st on needle over "k2tog" st. Fasten off.

Small Petal: (Make 3) Work Rows 1–10 of large petal, BO as for Row 15.

With tail threaded on a tapestry needle, pick up loops of CO edge and gather all 5 large petals tog. With same yarn, join the 3 small petals tog and tie to center of 5-petal group back. Fasten off. Work seven French knots (page 203) in center. Work 3-st knit cord (page 149) for stem. Add leaves, if desired.

Pansy

Small Petal: (Make 3) With CC, CO 3 sts.

Row 1: *K1f&b; rep from *, k1—5 sts.

Row 2: Change to MC and purl.

Row 3: *K1, CO 1; rep from *, end k1—9 sts.

Rows 4 and 8: Purl.

Row 5: K1 with CC2, k2 with MC, k1 with CC2, k2 with MC, k2 with CC2.

Row 6: P2 with CC2, p1 with MC, p3 with CC2, p1 with MC, p2 with CC2.

Row 7: With CC2, k2, *CO 1, k1; rep from *—15 sts.

Row 9: *Ssk, knit to last 2 sts, k2tog—13 sts.

Row 10: BO in purl.

Large petal: (Make 2 of MC) Work Rows 1–6 as for small petal, omitting color changes—9 sts.

Row 7: K1 *CO 1, k1; rep from *—17 sts.

Rows 8, 9, and 10: Work in St st.

Rows 11 and 13: *Ssk, knit to last 2 sts, k2tog—13 sts after Row 13.

Row 12: Purl.

Row 14: BO in purl.

Appliqué

With tail threaded on a tapestry needle, pick up CO loops of 3 small petals, pull tight and knot in back. Rep for 2 large petals. Place large petals behind small ones and sew in place.

Plumeria

With one color make 5 large Pansy petals (page 29), inc to 11 sts. Run threaded needle through CO sts of all petals; pull tight and knot in back. With CC, make French knot (page 203) in center, wrapping yarn around needle 5 times. Add leaves, if desired.

Basic Petal II

Petals are worked from outer edge to flower center. They are left on the needle and then rem sts are knit tog and dec'd to the center.

CO 5 sts.

Row 1: (RS) Knit.

Rows 2, 4, 6, 8, and 10: Purl.

Rows 3, 5, and 7: K1f&b each end of needle—11 sts after Row 7. (If you want to lengthen the petal, work 3 or 5 rows even.)

Rows 9 and 11: Dec 1 st each end of needle—7 sts rem after Row 11.

Row 12: P2tog, p3, p2og—5 sts.

Leave sts on needle. Rep for desired number of petals, leaving all sts on needle. When all petals are completed, k2tog across all sts on needle. Cut yarn leaving 12" (30.5-cm) tail. With tapestry needle, thread tail through rem sts on needle. Gather up and fasten securely.

Basic Flower Blossom

(Make 5) Work Rows 1–12 of Basic Petal II (above). With same needle, rep for each petal—25 sts total.

Row 7: *K2tog; rep from *, end k1—13 sts.

Row 8: *P2tog; rep from *, end p1—7 sts.

Pass last 6 sts over the 1st st—1 st. Fasten off.

Embroider stemmed French knots (page 203) in flower center.

Anemone

(Make 7) Work Rows 1–12 of Basic Petal II (page 30), working last 2 dec rows with CC for flower center. Leave sts on needle. Then k2tog across all sts. Cut yarn leaving 12" (30.5-cm) tail. With tapestry needle, thread tail through rem sts on needle. Gather up and fasten securely. Embroider French knot (page 203) in center. Add leaves, if desired.

Basic Petal III

Petals are knit separately and can be used free-form or applied to a background. This type of petal is good for poinsettias, daisies, and other flowers with overlapping petals.

Large petal: CO 3 sts. Work in St st, inc 1 st each end of needle every RS row until there are 9 sts. Work even for 8 rows, ending with a WS row. Dec as follows:

Row 1: (RS) Ssk, knit to last 2 sts, k2tog—2 sts dec'd.

Row 2: Purl.

Rep Rows 1 and 2 until 3 sts rem. Sl 1, k2tog, psso—1 st. Fasten off.

Small petal: CO 3 sts. Work in St st, inc 1 st each end of needle every other row until there are 9 sts. Work even for 4 rows, ending with a WS row. Rep Rows 1 and 2 above until 3 sts rem. Sl 1, k2tog, psso—1 st. Fasten off.

Columbine

Work Basic Petal III (page 31) 5 times. With tapestry needle, thread tail through rem st on each petal. Gather up and fasten securely. With CC1 and using the knitted method (page 259), CO 6 sts, *BO 5 sts, knit CO 5 sts; rep from * for each petal, end BO 5, fasten off. Form into a circle and sew to center of flower. With CC2, work 3 French knots (page 203) in flower center, wrapping yarn 3 times around needle.

Daisy

Bobble: CO 1 st. ([k1f&b] 2 times, k1) in same st. Turn, [p5, turn, k5, turn] 2 times, p5, turn, pass 2nd, 3rd, 4th, 5th, and 6th st over 1st st. Fasten off.

Work Basic Petal III (page 31) 7 times. With tapestry needle, thread tail through rem st on each petal. Gather up and fasten securely. Sew to background. With CC1, make bobble and sew to center of flower. With CC2, embroider stem st (page 193) for stalk and leaves.

Picot Chain Flower

In groups, these petals make beautiful lilacs or hyacinths.

Make a slip knot and place on left needle. *CO 3 sts. BO 3 sts. Place rem loop on left needle. Make another petal the same way in rem loop. Rep from * 5 times—6 petals. Join the petals into a circle by picking up and knitting 1 st into the original slip knot. BO 1 st and fasten off. Work French knot (page 203) in flower center, wrapping yarn 3 times around needle. Note: To make a larger flower, CO and BO more sts.

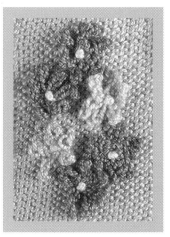

Poinsettia

Petal: (make 10) CO 3 sts. Work in St st, inc 1 st each end of needle every other row until there are 9 sts. Work even for 1" (2.5 cm), ending with a WS row.

Rows 1, 3, and 5: Ssk, knit to last 2 sts, k2tog—3 sts rem after Row 5.

Rows 2, 4, and 6: Purl.

Row 7: Sl 1, k2tog, psso—1 st. Fasten off.

Leaf: (make 2) CO 5 sts.

Row 1: K2, yo, k1, yo, k2—7 sts.

Rows 2, 4, 6, and 8: Purl.

Row 3: K3, yo, k1, yo, k3—9 sts.

Row 5: K2tog, k5, k2tog—7 sts.

Row 7: K2tog, k3, k2tog—5 sts.

Row 9: K2tog, k1, k2tog—3 sts.

Row 10: Sl 1, k2tog, psso—1 st. Fasten off.

Bobble: (Make 7) CO 1 st. ([K1f&b] 2 times, k1) in same st—5 sts. Work 4 rows St st. Pass last 4 sts over 1st st. Fasten off.

Arrange 5 petals in star shape. Arrange rem 5 petals on top of and offset from first 5 petals and sew in place. Attach leaves. Attach bobbles to flower center so that rev St st faces outward.

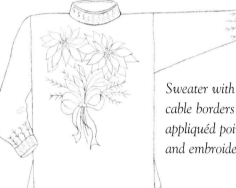

Sweater with cable borders, appliquéd poinsettias, and embroidery.

Bobble Flower

Bobble: CO 1 st, leaving 6" (15-cm) tail.

Row 1: ([K1f&b] 2 times, k1) in same st—5 sts.

Rows 2, 4, and 6: Purl.

Rows 3 and 5: Knit.

Row 7: K2tog, k1, k2tog—3 sts.

Row 8: P3tog—1 st. Fasten off.

Make a total of 9 bobbles. Arrange 8 in a circle around the 9th. Sew in place so that CO end touches BO end of each bobble. Add leaves, if desired.

Daisy Bobble Flower

Work 7 bobbles as for Bobble Flower (page 33). Arrange 6 bobbles in a circle around the 7th. Sew in place so that CO end touches BO end of center bobble only, and so that the 6 outer bobbles are elongated. Add leaves and stem, if desired.

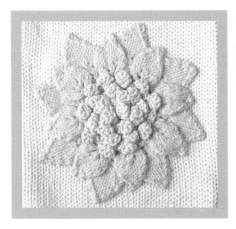

Sunflower

Large Petals: (Make 8) Work as for large leaf (page 35).
Small Petals (Make 8) Work as for medium leaf (page 36).
Bobble center: CO 99 sts. Work rev St st bobble cord (page 152) for desired length for flower center.

Arrange large petals in circle and sew to knitted background. Sew small petals on top of large ones. Shape bobble cord into a spiral in the center and sew in place.

Beaded Loop Flower

Materials: #5 cotton; 1 vial seed beads; 1 vial CC seed beads; beading needle.

Needles: 1.5 mm dpn; tapestry needle.
See page 262–263 for bead and beaded knitting instructions.
SB1: Slip designated number of beads, in this case 1, next to last st made on right needle.
BK1: Insert the needle into the stitch to be knitted as usual, slide the bead up against the needle, and pull the bead through to the front as you complete the stitch.
BP1: Work as for BK1, but purl the stitch instead of knitting it.
Notes: When knitting 2tog, do so with a bead. Maintain an edge st on each end and work rem sts in bead knitting.
Preparation: String beads onto knitting yarn (page 262).

CO 54 sts.

Rows 1 and 3: K1, [BK1] 2 times, *SB11, k1, [BK1] 2 times; rep from *; end last rep [BK1] 3 times, k1.

Rows 2, 4, 6, 8, 10, and 12: P1, BP to last st, p1.

Row 5: K1, BK1, *SB11, k2tog, BK1; rep from *, end k1—37 sts.

Row 7: K1, BK1, *SB9, k2tog, BK1; rep from *, end BK1, k1—26 sts.

Row 9: K1, BK1, *SB9, k2tog, BK1; rep from *, end SB9, k2tog, k1—18 sts.

Row 11: K1, BK1, *SB7, k2tog; rep from *, end BK1, k1—11 sts.

Row 13: Change to CC beads. K1, *k2tog; rep from *—6 sts.

Row 14: Rep Row 2 with CC beads.

Cut yarn leaving 12" (30.5-cm) tail. With tapestry needle, thread tail through rem sts on needle. Gather up and fasten securely. Sew seam.

Leaves

The following leaves were inspired by autumn walks along the streets of New York and Paris. I gathered and pressed many beautiful leaves, then chose my favorites and duplicated them in knit stitches. I've taken poetic license with some of the names. All are shaped with increases, decreases, and basic stitches. When making leaves, don't hesitate to use non-traditional colors and variegated or textured yarns.

Aspen Leaf

Work this leaf in two (or more) colors for variation.

Large: CO 5 sts.

Row 1: (RS) K2, yo, k1, yo, k2—7 sts.

Row 2 and all even-numbered rows: Purl.

Row 3: K3, yo, k1, yo, k3—9 sts.

Row 5: K4, yo, k1, yo, k4—11 sts.

Row 7: K5, yo, k1, yo, k5—13 sts.

Row 9: Ssk, k9, k2tog—11 sts.

Row 11: Ssk, k7, k2tog—9 sts.

Row 13: Ssk, k5, k2tog—7 sts.

Row 15: Ssk, k3, k2tog—5 sts.

Row 17: Ssk, k1, k2tog—3 sts.

Row 19: Sl 1, k2tog, psso—1 st. Fasten off.

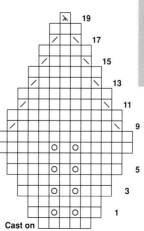

Appliqué

Medium: CO 5 sts.
Row 1: (RS) K2, yo, k1, yo, k2—7 sts.
Row 2 and all even-numbered rows: Purl.
Row 3: K3, yo, k1, yo, k3—9 sts.
Row 5: K4, yo, k1, yo, k4—11 sts.
Row 7: Ssk, k7, k2tog—9 sts.
Row 9: Ssk, k5, k2tog—7 sts.
Row 11: Ssk, k3, k2tog—5 sts.
Row 13: Ssk, k1, k2tog—3 sts.
Row 15: Sl 1, k2tog, psso—1 st. Fasten off.

Small: CO 5 sts.
Row 1: (RS) K2, yo, k1, yo, k2—7 sts.
Row 2 and all even-numbered rows: Purl.
Row 3: K3, yo, k1, yo, k3—9 sts.
Row 5: Ssk, k5, k2tog—7 sts.
Row 7: Ssk, k3, k2tog—5 sts.
Row 9: Ssk, k1, k2tog—3 sts.
Row 11: Sl 1, k2tog, psso—1 st. Fasten off.

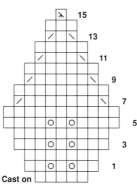

Medium

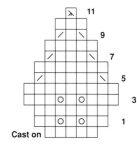

Small

Extra Small: CO 5 sts.
Row 1: (RS) K2, yo, k1, yo, k2—7 sts.
Rows 2, 4, and 6: Purl.
Row 3: Ssk, k3, k2tog—5 sts.
Row 5: Ssk, k1, k2tog—3 sts.
Row 7: Sl 1, k2tog, psso—1 st. Fasten off.

Pullover decorated with appliquéd leaves, knit cord, bobbles, and embroidery, and edged with fence rib.

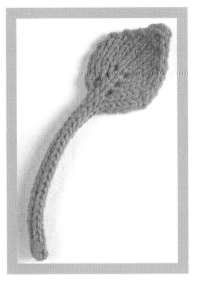

Leaf on a Stem

CO 4 sts. Work knit cord (page 149) until piece measures 4" (10 cm), inc 1 st on last row—5 sts. Do not BO. Work leaf as follows:

Row 1: (RS) K2, yo, k1, yo, k2—7 sts.

Rows 2, 4, 6, 8, 10, and 12: (WS) Purl.

Row 3: K3, yo, k1, yo, k3—9 sts.

Row 5: K4, yo, k1, yo, k4—11 sts.

Row 7: Ssk, k7, k2tog—9 sts.

Row 9: Ssk, k5, k2tog—7 sts.

Row 11: Ssk, k3, k2tog—5 sts.

Row 13: Ssk, k1, k2tog—3 sts.

Row 14: Sl 1 pwise, p2tog, psso—1 st.
  Fasten off.

Leaf Trio on a Stem

Work Leaf on a Stem (above) through Row 5—11 sts.

Rows 6–10: Work in St st.

Row 11: Ssk, k7, k2tog—9 sts.

Rows 12, 14, and 16: Purl.

Row 13: Ssk, k5, k2tog—7 sts.

Row 15: Ssk, k3, k2tog—5 sts.

Row 17: Ssk, k1, k2tog—3 sts.

Row 18: Sl 1 pwise, p2tog,
  psso—1 st. Fasten off.

  Work 2 more single leaves (as above) and then sew to each side of stem near first leaf.

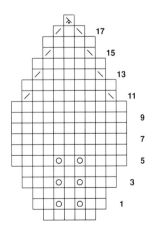

Basic Leaf with Vertical Eyelets

Work in tweed yarn or multiple colors for an autumn look.

CO 5 sts.
Row 1: (RS) K2, yo, k1, yo, k2—7 sts.
Rows 2, 4, and 6: Purl.
Row 3: K3, yo, k1, yo, k3—9 sts.
Row 5: K4, yo, k1, yo, k4—11 sts.
Row 7: BO 3 sts, [k1, yo] 2 times, k5—10 sts.
Row 8: BO 3 sts, p6—7 sts.
Row 9: K3, yo, k1, yo, k3—9 sts.
Rows 10, 12, and 16: Purl.
Row 11: K4, yo, k1, yo, k4—11 sts.
Row 13: BO 3 sts, k7—8 sts.
Row 14: BO 3 sts, p4—5 sts.
Row 15: Ssk, k1, k2tog—3 sts.
Row 17: Sl 1, k2tog, psso—1 st. Fasten off.

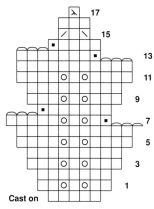

Two-Color Variation

With A CO 5 sts.
Row 1: (RS) K2, yo, k1, yo, k2—7 sts.
Row 2: With A, purl.
Row 3: With A, k3, yo, k1, yo, join B and k3—9 sts.
Row 4: With B, p4, with A, p5.
Row 5: With A, k4, yo, k1, yo, with B, k4—11 sts.
Row 6: With B, p5, with A, p6.
Row 7: With A, BO 3 sts, [k1, yo] 2 times, with B, k5—10 sts.
Row 8: With B, BO 3 sts, p1, with A, p5—7 sts.
Row 9: With A, k3, [yo, k1] 2 times, with B, k2—9 sts.
Row 10: With B, p3, with A, p6.

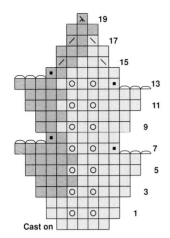

Row 11: With A, k4, [yo, k1] 2 times, with B, k3—11 sts.

Row 12: With B, p4, with A, p7.

Row 13: With A, BO 3 sts, [k1, yo] 2 times, k1, with B, k4—10 sts.

Row 14: With B, BO 3 sts, p1, with A, p5—7 sts.

Row 15: With A, ssk, k2, with B, k1, k2tog—5 sts.

Row 16: With B, p3, with A, p2.

Row 17: With A, ssk, with B, k1, k2tog—3 sts.

Row 18: With B, p3.

Row 19: Sl 1, k2tog, psso—1 st. Fasten off.

Basic Leaf with Diagonal Eyelets

CO 5 sts.

Row 1: (RS) K2, yo, k1, yo, k2—7 sts.

Rows 2, 4, and 6: Purl.

Row 3: K2, yo, k3, yo, k2—9 sts.

Row 5: K2, yo, k5, yo, k2—11 sts.

Row 7: BO 3 sts, [k1, yo] 2 times, k5—10 sts.

Row 8: BO 3 sts, p6—7 sts.

Row 9: K2, yo, k3, yo, k2—9 sts.

Rows 10, 12, and 16: Purl.

Row 11: K2, yo, k5, yo, k2—11 sts.

Row 13: BO 3 sts, k7—8 sts.

Row 14: BO 3 sts, p4—5 sts.

Row 15: Ssk, k1, k2tog—3 sts.

Row 17: Sl 1, k2tog, psso—1 st. Fasten off.

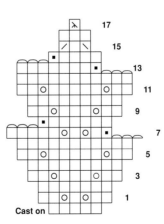

Garter-Stitch Leaf

Small: CO 9 sts.

Rows 1, 3, and 5: K3, sl 2tog kwise, k1, p2sso, k3—7 sts.

Rows 2 and 4: K1, M1, k2, p1, k2, M1, k1—9 sts.

Row 6: K3, p1, k3.

Row 7: K2, sl 2tog kwise, k1, p2sso, k2—5 sts.

Row 8: K2, p1, k2.

Row 9: K1, sl 2tog kwise, k1, p2sso, k1—3 sts.

Row 10: K1, p1, k1.

Row 11: Sl 2tog kwise, k1, p2sso—1 st. Fasten off.

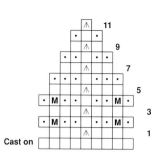

Medium: CO 15 sts.

Row 1: K6, sl 2tog kwise, k1, p2sso, k6—13 sts.

Row 2: K6, p1, k6.

Row 3: K5, sl 2tog kwise, k1, p2sso, k5—11 sts.

Row 4: K5, p1, k5.

Row 5: K4, sl 2tog kwise, k1, p2sso, k4—9 sts.

Row 6: K4, p1, k4.

Row 7: K3, sl 2tog kwise, k1, p2sso, k3—7 sts.

Row 8: K3, p1, k3.

Row 9: K2, sl 2tog kwise, k1, p2sso, k2—5 sts.

Row 10: K2, p1, k2.

Row 11: K1, sl 2tog kwise, k1, p2sso, k1—3 sts.

Row 12: K1, p1, k1.

Row 13: Sl 2tog kwise, k1, p2sso—1 st. Fasten off.

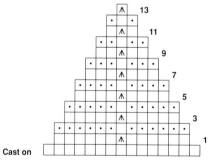

Poplar Leaf

CO 2 sts.

Row 1: K1, M1, k1—3 sts.

Rows 2, 4, 6, 8, and 12: Purl.

Row 3: K1, [M1, k1] 2 times—5 sts.

Row 5: K1, [M1, k1] 4 times—9 sts.

Row 7: [K2, M1] 2 times, k1, [M1, k2] 2 times—13 sts.

Row 9: BO 2 sts, k10—11 sts.

Row 10: BO 2 sts, p8—9 sts.

Row 11: Knit.

Rows 13–24: Rep Rows 7–12 two times.

Row 25: Ssk, k5, k2tog—7 sts.

Row 26: P2tog, p3, ssp—5 sts.

Row 27: Ssk, k1, k2tog—3 sts.

Row 28: Sl 1 pwise, p2tog, psso—1 st. Fasten off.

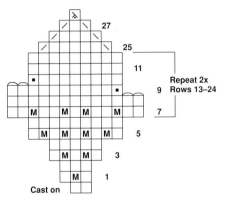

Oriental Leaf

Small: CO 2 sts.

Row 1: K1, M1, k1—3 sts.

Rows 2, 4, 6, 10, 12, and 16: Purl.

Row 3: K1, [M1, k1] 2 times—
5 sts.

Rows 5 and 11: K1, [M1, k1]
4 times—9 sts.

Rows 7 and 13: BO 2 sts, k6—
7 sts.

Rows 8 and 14: BO 2 sts, k4—5 sts.

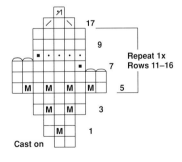

Rows 9 and 15: Knit.

Row 17: Ssk, k1, k2tog—3 sts.

Row 18: P3tog—1 st. Fasten off.

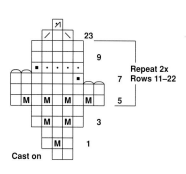

Large: CO 2 sts.

Row 1: K1, M1, k1—3 sts.

Rows 2, 4, 6, 8, 10, 12, 16, 18, and 22: Purl.

Row 3: K1, [M1, k1] 2 times—5 sts.

Rows 5, 11, and 17: K1, [M1, k1] 4 times—9 sts.

Row 7, 13, and 19: BO 2 sts, k6—7 sts.

Row 8, 14, and 20: BO 2 sts, k4—5 sts.

Row 9, 15, and 21: Knit.

Row 23: Ssk, k1, k2tog—3 sts.

Row 24: P3tog—1 st. Fasten off.

Elm Leaf with Vertical Eyelets

CO 5 sts. Work St st for 4 rows.

Row 1: (RS) K1f&b, k2, yo, k1, yo, k2, k1f&b—11 sts.

Row 2 and all even-numbered rows except 8, 14, and 20: Purl.

Rows 3 and 9: K4, yo, k1, yo, k4.

Rows 5 and 11: K5, yo, k1, yo, k5—13 sts.

Rows 7 and 13: BO 3 sts, k2, yo, k1, yo, k6—12 sts.

Rows 8 and 14: BO 3 sts, p8—9 sts.

Row 15: K4, yo, k1, yo, k4—11 sts.

Row 17: K5, yo, k1, yo, k5—13 sts.

Row 19: BO 3 sts, k9—10 sts.

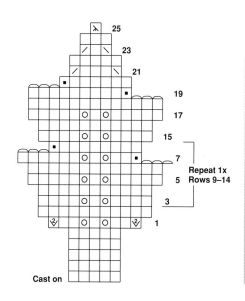

Row 20: BO 3 sts, p6—7 sts.
Row 21: Ssk, k3, k2tog—5 sts.
Row 23: Ssk, k1, k2tog—3 sts.
Row 25: Sl 1, k2tog, psso—1 st.
  Fasten off.

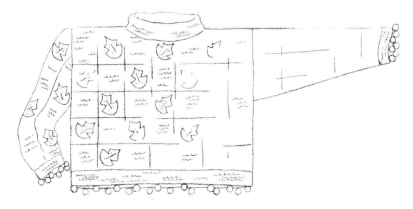

Pullover worked in blocks of stockinette stitch and reverse stockinette stitch, edged with reverse stockinette stitch and bobbles, and appliquéd with leaves.

Elm Leaf with Diagonal Eyelets

CO 7 sts.
Row 1: (RS) K3, yo, k1, yo, k3—9 sts.
Row 2 and all even-numbered rows except 8, 14, and 20: Purl.
Rows 3 and 9: K3, yo, k3, yo, k3—11 sts.
Rows 5 and 11: K3, yo, k5, yo, k3—13 sts.
Rows 7 and 13: BO 3 sts, k2, yo, k1, yo, k6—12 sts.
Rows 8 and 14: BO 3 sts, p8—9 sts.
Row 15: K3, yo, k3, yo, k3—11 sts.
Row 17: K3, yo, k5, yo, k3—13 sts.
Row 19: BO 4 sts, [k1, yo] 2 times, k6—11 sts.
Row 20: BO 4 sts, p6—7 sts.
Row 21: Ssk, yo, sl 2tog kwise, k1, p2sso, yo, k2tog—5 sts.
Row 23: Ssk, k1, k2tog—3 sts.
Row 25: Sl 1, k2tog, psso—1 st.
  Fasten off.

Seed-Stitch Leaf

CO 3 sts.

Row 1: K1, p1, k1—3 sts.

Row 2: K1f&b, p1, k1f&b—5 sts.

Row 3: [P1, k1] 2 times, p1.

Row 4: K1f&b, k1, p1, k1, k1f&b—7 sts.

Row 5: [K1, p1] 3 times, k1.

Row 6: K1f&b, [p1, k1] 2 times, p1, k1f&b—9 sts.

Row 7: [P1, k1] 4 times, p1.

Rows 8, 14, and 20: K1f&b, [k1, p1] 3 times, k1, k1f&b—11 sts.

Rows 9, 15, and 21: [K1, p1] 5 times, k1.

Rows 10, 16, and 22: K1f&b, [p1, k1] 4 times, p1, k1f&b—13 sts.

Rows 11, 17, and 23: BO 2 sts, [k1, p1] 5 times—11 sts.

Row 12, 18, and 24: BO 2 sts, [k1, p1] 4 times—9 sts.

Rows 13, 19, and 25: [P1, k1] 4 times, p1.

Row 26: P2tog, [p1, k1] 2 times, p1, ssp—7 sts.

Row 27: K2tog, k1, p1, k1, ssk—5 sts.

Row 28: p2tog, p1, ssp—3 sts.

Row 29: Sl 1, p2tog, psso—1 st. Fasten off.

Embroider stem st (page 193) for veins.

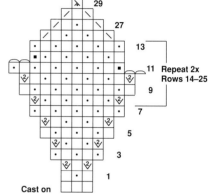

Elegant Oak

CO 5 sts. Work knit cord (page 149) until piece measures 1¼" (3.2 cm).

Row 1: K1, M1, [k1, yo] 2 times, k1, M1, k1—9 sts.

Row 2 and all even-numbered rows except 12, 22, and 36: Purl.

Rows 3, 13, and 23: [K3, yo] 2 times, k3—11 sts.

Rows 5, 15, and 25: K3, yo, k5, yo, k3—13 sts.

Rows 7 and 17: K3, yo, k7, yo, k3—15 sts.

Rows 9 and 19: K3, yo, k9, yo, k3—17 sts.

Rows 11 and 21: K8, yo, k1, yo, k3, sl last 5 sts onto holder—14 sts.

Rows 12 and 22: P9, sl last 5 sts onto holder—9 sts.

Row 27: Ssk, k1, yo, k2tog, k3, ssk, yo, k1, k2tog—11 sts.

Row 29: Ssk, yo, k2tog, k3, ssk, yo, k2tog—9 sts.

Row 31: Ssk, yo, k2tog, k1, ssk, yo, k2tog—7 sts.

Row 33: Ssk, yo, sl 2tog kwise, k1, p2sso, yo, k2tog—5 sts.

Row 35: K1, sl 2tog kwise, k1, p2sso, k1—3 sts.

Row 36: Sl 1 pwise, p2tog, psso—1 st. Fasten off.

With RS facing, place sts from upper left holder onto needle. Join yarn.

Row 1: Knit.

Rows 2 and 4: Purl.

Row 3: Ssk, k1, k2tog—3 sts.

Row 5: Sl 2tog kwise, k1, p2sso—1 st. Fasten off. Rep for sts on lower left holder.

With RS facing, place sts from upper right holder onto needle. Join yarn.

Row 1: Ssk, k1, k2tog—3 sts.

Row 2: Purl.

Row 3: Sl 2tog kwise, k1, p2sso—1 st.

Fasten off. Rep for sts on lower right holder.

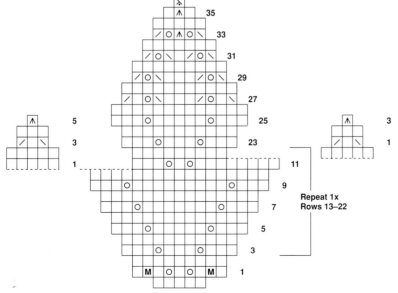

Tristan's Picot Leaf

(Worked from the top down)

Using the provisional method (page 259), CO 21 sts.

Rows 1, 3, 5, and 7: Knit.

Rows 2 and 6: Purl.

Row 4: (Picot row) P1, *yo, p2tog; rep from *.

Row 8: (WS) Place live CO sts on a spare dpn and place in front of and parallel to working needle. Fold at picot row. P2tog (1 st from each needle) across row—21 sts.

Row 9: K1, [p1, k1b] 4 times, sl 1 kwise, k2tog, psso, [k1b, p1] 4 times, k1—19 sts.

Row 10: P1, [k1, p1b] 3 times, k1, sl 1 pwise, p2tog, psso, k1, [p1b, k1] 3 times, p1—17 sts.

Row 11: K1, [p1, k1b] 3 times, sl 1 kwise, k2tog, psso, [k1b, p1] 3 times, k1—15 sts.

Row 12: P1, [k1, p1b] 2 times, k1, sl 1 pwise, p2tog, psso, k1, [p1b, k1] 2 times, p1—13 sts.

Row 13: K1, [p1, k1b] 2 times, sl 1 kwise, k2tog, psso, [k1b, p1] 2 times, k1—11 sts.

Row 14: P1, k1, p1b, k1, sl 1 pwise, p2tog, psso, k1, p1b, k1, p1—9 sts.

Row 15: K1, p1, k1b, sl 1 kwise, k2tog, psso, k1b, p1, k1—7 sts.

Row 16: P1, k1, sl 1 pwise, p2tog, psso, k1, p1—5 sts. Change to dpn.

Row 17: K1, sl 1 kwise, k2tog, psso, k1—3 sts.

Work rem sts in knit cord (page 149) for 1½" (3.8 cm). K3tog—1 st. Fasten off.

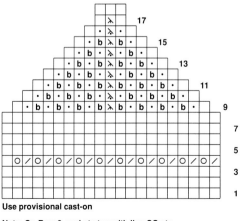

Use provisional cast-on

Note: On Row 8, purl sts tog with live CO sts.

Sonja's Leaf

CO 5 sts. Work knit cord (page 149) until piece measures ¾" (2 cm).

Row 1: (RS) K2, M1, k1, M1, k2—7 sts.

Row 2 and all even-numbered rows except 16, 22, and 28: Purl.

Row 3: K3, M1, k1, M1, k3—9 sts.

Rows 5–14: Cont inc 1 st after the first 3 sts and before the last 3 sts every other row in this manner—19 sts after Row 13.

Row 15: BO 3 sts, k5, M1, k1, M1, k9—18 sts.

Row 16: BO 3 sts, purl to end—15 sts.

Row 17: K7, M1, k1, M1, k7—17 sts.

Row 19: K8, M1, k1, M1, k8—19 sts.

Row 21: BO 3 sts, knit to end—16 sts.

Row 22: BO 3 sts, purl to end—13 sts.

Rows 23 and 25: Knit.

Row 27: BO 3 sts, knit to end—10 sts.

Row 28: BO 3 sts, purl to end—7 sts.

Row 29: Ssk, k3, k2tog—5 sts.

Row 31: Ssk, k1, k2tog—3 sts.

Row 33: Sl 1, k2tog, psso—1 st. Fasten off.

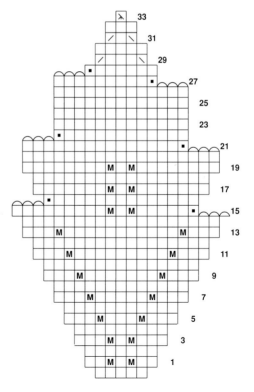

Leaf Derickson

CO 5 sts. Work tube st (page 151) for 1" (2.5 cm).

Row 1: (RS) [K1, M1] 2 times, p1, [M1, k1] 2 times—9 sts.

Row 2 and all even-numbered rows except 26 and 28: Knit the knits and purl the purls.

Row 3: 2/2RC, M1 pwise, p1, M1 pwise, 2/2LC—11 sts.

Row 5: K4, M1 pwise, p3, M1 pwise, k4—13 sts.

Row 7: 2/2RC, M1 pwise, p5, M1 pwise, 2/2LC—15 sts.

Row 9: K4, M1 pwise, p7, M1 pwise, k4—17 sts.

Row 11: 2/2RC, M1 pwise, p9, M1 pwise, 2/2LC—19 sts.

Rows 13, 17, and 21: Knit the knits and purl the purls.

Row 15: 2/2RC, p2tog, p7, ssp, 2/2LC—17 sts.

Row 19: 2/2RC, p2tog, p5, ssp, 2/2LC—15 sts.

Row 23: 2/2RC, p2tog, p3, ssp, 2/2LC—13 sts.

Row 26: P4, sl 1 pwise, p2tog, psso, p4—9 sts.

Row 27: Sl 2 sts onto cn and hold in back, [k1 from left needle tog with 1 st on cn] 2 times, p1, sl 2 sts onto cn and hold in front, [k1 from cn tog with 1 st on left needle] 2 times—5 sts.

Row 28: P1, sl 1 pwise, p2tog, psso, p1—3 sts.

Row 29: Sl 1, k2tog, psso—1 st. Fasten off.

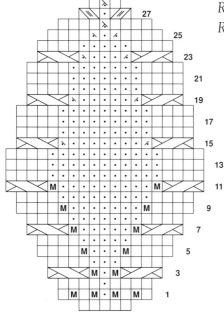

Purl all M1 stitches on all rows except Row 1.

Lancelot's Leaf

Note: Slip marker on all rows.

CO 3 sts.

Row 1: (RS) K1, M1, k1, pm, M1, k1—5 sts.

Row 2 and all even-numbered rows: Knit to m, yf, sl 1 pwise, yb, knit to end.

Row 3: K1, M1, knit to last st, M1, k1—7 sts.

Rows 5, 7, 9, 11, 13, 15, and 17: Rep Row 3, working M1 incs after the first and before the last st—21 sts after Row 17.

Row 19: [K2tog] 5 times, k1, [k2tog] 5 times—11 sts.

Row 21: [K2tog] 2 times, sl 2 tog kwise, k1, p2sso, [k2tog] 2 times—5 sts.

Row 23: Change to dpn. K2tog, k1, k2tog—3 sts.

Maintaining sl st on every other row as established, cont working knit cord (page 149) for 2" (5 cm). K3tog—1 st. Fasten off.

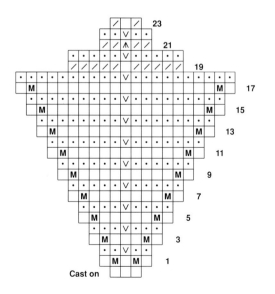

Felted Leaves

Any leaf made from wool can be felted. See page 263 for felting instructions.

Vine with Leaves

Work Leaf on a Stem (page 37). Then work 6 more single leaves and sew to stem as desired.

Beaded Leaf

Materials: #5 perle cotton; 1 vial seed beads; beading needle.

Needles: Size 000 (1.5 mm) dpn; tapestry needle.

BK1: Insert the needle into the stitch to be knitted as usual, slide the bead up against the needle, and pull the bead through to the front as you complete the stitch.

BP1: Work as for BK1, but purl the stitch instead of knitting it.

Note: Maintain an edge st on each end and work rem sts in bead knitting. See pages 262–263 for instructions on knitting with beads.

Preparation: Thread beads onto the knitting yarn (see page 262).

CO 5 sts. Work tube st (page 151) for ½" (1.3 cm).

Note: For all single-st CO, use the backward loop method (page 260) and work a bead into the st.

Row 1: (RS) K1, [BK1, CO 1] 2 times, BK1, k1— 7 sts.

Row 2 and all even-numbered rows: P1, BP1 to last st, p1.

Row 3: K1, BK1, CO 1, [BK1] 3 times, CO 1, BK1, k1—9 sts.

Row 5: K1, [BK1, CO 1] 2 times, [BK1] 3 times, [CO 1, BK1] 2 times, k1—13 sts.

Row 7: K1, [BK1, CO 1] 3 times, [BK1] 3 times, [CO 1, BK1] 3 times, k1—17 sts.

Rows 9, 11, and 13: K1, BK1 to last st, k1.

Row 15: Ssk, BK1 to last 2 sts, k2tog.

Cont to dec in this manner every other row until 3 sts rem, ending with a WS row. Sl 2tog kwise, k1, p2sso. Fasten off.

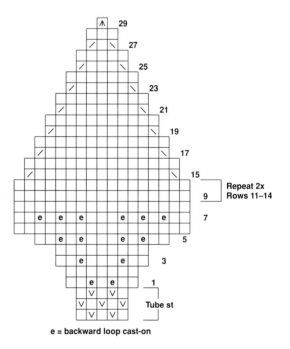

e = backward loop cast-on

Appliqué

Vain Leaf

CO 7 sts.

Row 1: K1, M1, k1, yo, M1, yo, sl 2tog kwise, k1, p2sso, yo, M1, yo, k1, M1, k1—13 sts.

Row 2 and all even-numbered rows except 8, 16, and 24: Purl.

Rows 3 and 11: K3, yo, k2, yo, sl 2tog kwise, k1, p2sso, yo, k2, yo, k3— 15 sts.

Rows 5 and 13: [K3, yo] 2 times, sl 2tog kwise, k1, p2sso, [yo, k3] 2 times—17 sts.

Rows 7 and 15: BO 3 sts, k3, yo, sl 2tog kwise, k1, p2sso, yo, k7— 14 sts.

Rows 8 and 16: BO 3 sts, p10—11 sts.

Row 9: K3, yo, k1, yo, sl 2tog kwise, k1, p2sso, yo, k1, yo, k3—13 sts.

Row 17: Ssk, k2, yo, sl 2tog kwise, k1, p2sso, yo, k2, k2tog—9 sts.

Row 19: Ssk, k1, yo, sl 2tog kwise, k1, p2sso, yo, k1, k2tog—7 sts.

Row 21: Ssk, yo, sl 2tog kwise, k1, p2sso, yo, k2tog—5 sts.

Row 23: Ssk, k1, k2tog—3 sts.

Row 24: P3tog—1 st. Fasten off.

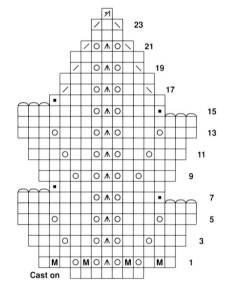

Large Gold Leaf

CO 5 sts. Work tube st (page 151) until piece measures 1"
   (2.5 cm).

Row 1: (RS) *K1, M1; rep from *, end k1—9 sts.

Rows 2, 4, 6, and 8: Purl.

Row 3: *K1, M1; rep from *, end k1—17 sts.

Row 5: *K1, M1; rep from *, end k1—33 sts.

Row 7: Knit.

Row 9: BO 3 sts, knit to end.

Row 10: BO 3 sts, purl to end.

Rows 11–14: Work in St st.

Rows 15–26: Rep Rows 9–14 twice.

Rows 27–28: Rep Rows 9–10.

Rows 29–30: Work in St st.

Rows 31–32: Rep Rows 9–10.

Rows 33–34: Work in St st.

Row 35: Sl 1, k2tog, psso—1 st.
   Fasten off.

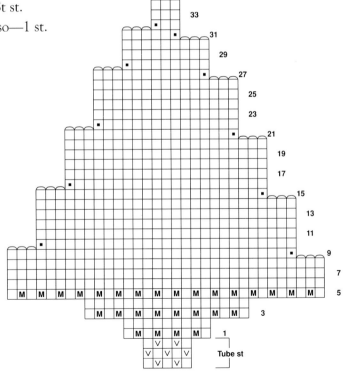

Appliqué

Small Gold Leaf

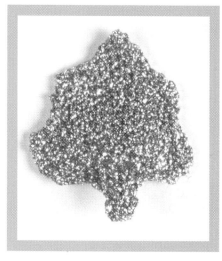

CO 5 sts. Work tube st (page 151) for 1" (2.5 cm).

Row 1: (RS) *K1, M1; rep from *, end k1—9 sts.

Rows 2, 4, 6, 10, 12, and 16: Purl.

Row 3: *K1, M1; rep from *,
end k1—17 sts.

Row 5: Knit.

Row 7: BO 3 sts, knit to
end—14 sts.

Row 8: BO 3 sts, purl to
end—11 sts.

Rows 9 and 11: Knit.

Row 13: BO 3 sts, knit to
end—8 sts.

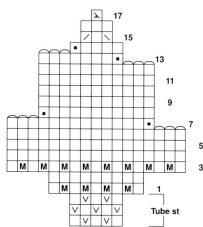

Row 14: BO 3 sts, purl to end—5 sts.

Row 15: Ssk, k1, k2tog—3 sts.

Row 17: Sl 1, k2tog, psso—1 st. Fasten off.

Maple Leaf

Note: Slip markers on all rows.

CO 7 sts.

Set-up row: (WS) P3, pm, sl 1 pwise, pm, p3.

Row 1: K1, M1, k2, yo, k1, yo, k2, M1, k1—11 sts.

Rows 2, 4, 6, 8, 10, and 12: Purl, slipping 1 pwise bet
markers.

Row 3: K1, M1, k4, yo, k1, yo, k4, M1, k1—15 sts.

Row 5: K7, yo, k1, yo, k7—17 sts.

Row 7: K8, yo, k1, yo, k8—19 sts.

Row 9: K9, yo, k1, yo, k9—21 sts.

Row 11: Knit.

Row 13: [K7, M1] 2 times, k2, place last 5 sts on holder—18 sts.

Row 14: P13, place last 5 sts on holder—13 sts.

Center: (Worked on center 13 sts)

Row 15: Knit.

Rows 16, 18, 20, 22, 24, and 26: Purl.

Row 17: K1, ssk, k7, k2tog, k1—11 sts.

Row 19: K1, ssk, k5, k2tog, k1—9 sts.

Row 21: K1, ssk, k3, k2tog, k1—7 sts.

Row 23: K1, ssk, k1, k2tog, k1—5 sts.

Row 25: K1, sl 1, k2tog, psso, k1—3 sts.

Row 27: Sl 1, k2tog, psso—1 st.

   Fasten off.

Right side: (Worked on first 5 sts)

Rows 14, 16, and 18: Purl.

Row 15: Knit.

Row 17: K1, sl 1, k2tog, psso, k1—3 sts.

Row 19: Sl 1, k2tog, psso,—1 st. Fasten off.

Left side: (Worked on rem 5 sts)

Rows 13 and 15: Knit.

Rows 14, 16, and 18: Purl.

Row 17: K1, sl 1, k2tog, psso, k1—3 sts.

Row 19: Sl 1, k2tog, psso—1 st. Fasten off.

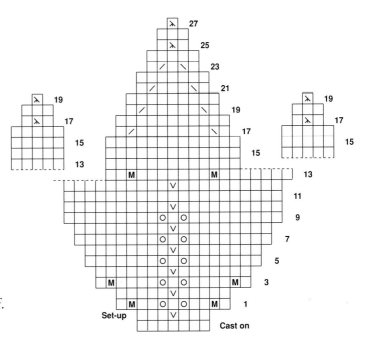

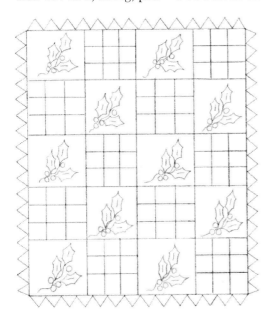

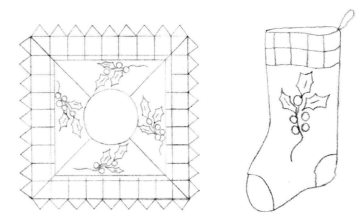

Afghan, tree skirt, and Christmas stocking embellished with appliquéd leaves, bobbles, and stem stitch. Tree skirt and afghan edged with a pointed border.

New Leaf

CO 6 sts.

Row 1: K4, yf, sl 1, yb, turn.

Row 2: Sl 1st st to right needle, yb, k3, k1f&b, turn—7 sts.

Rep Rows 1 and 2 until there are 15 sts. Work Row 1 again. Dec as follows:

Row 1: Sl 1st st to right needle, yb, k4, turn.

Row 2: K2tog, k3, yf, sl 1, yb, turn.

Rep dec Rows 1 and 2 until there are 6 sts. Then work Row 1 again. BO 5 sts—1 st. **Stem:** Using the cable method (page 259), CO 5 more sts, BO 5 sts. Fasten off.

Trees

The following trees are unique and have great design potential. I've given instructions for eyelet, garter, loop, cable, and bobble trees. Sew together triangles knitted with textured yarns for a country patchwork look. Be adventurous; decorate them with embroidery, beads, or rhinestones.

Pine Tree

Extra Large: CO 7 sts. Work k1, p1 rib until piece measures 1" (2.5 cm), ending with a WS row. Using the cable method (page 259), CO 12 sts—19 sts.

Row 1: (RS) Knit the 12 CO sts, then 7 rib sts, then cable CO 12 sts—31 sts.

Row 2 and all even-numbered rows except 20 and 36: Purl.

Row 3: K13, ssk, yo, k1, yo, k2tog, k13.

Row 5: K1, ssk, k10, ssk, yo, k1, yo, k2tog, k10, k2tog, k1—29 sts.

Row 7 and all odd-numbered rows through 19: Cont in patt, dec 1 st at beg and end of row as in Row 5—15 sts after Row 19.

Row 20: Purl, then cable CO 6 sts at end of row—21 sts.

Row 21: K11, ssk, yo, k1, yo, k2tog, k5, cable CO 6 sts—27 sts.

Row 23 and all odd-numbered rows through 35:
Cont in patt, dec 1 st at beg and end of
row as before—13 sts after Row 35.

Row 36: Purl, then cable CO 4 sts at end of
row—17 sts.

Row 37: K8, ssk, yo, k1, yo, k2tog, k4, cable
CO 4 sts—21 sts.

Row 39 and all odd-numbered rows through 49:
Cont in patt, dec 1 st at beg and end of
row as before—9 sts after Row 49.

Row 51: [Ssk] 2 times, yo, k1, yo, [k2tog]
2 times—7 sts.

Row 53: Ssk, sl 2tog kwise, k1, p2sso,
k2tog—3 sts.

Row 55: Sl 2tog kwise, k1, p2sso—1 st.
Fasten off.

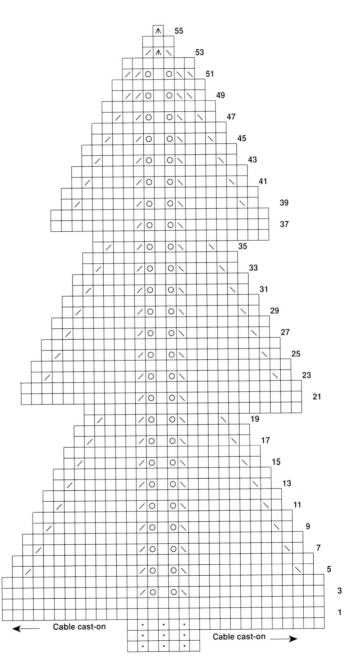

Appliqué

Large: CO 7 sts. Work in k1, p1 rib until piece measures 1" (2.5 cm), ending with a WS row. Using the cable method (page 259), CO 8 sts—15 sts.

Row 1: (RS) K15, cable CO 8 more sts—23 sts.

Row 2 and all even-numbered rows except 16 and 30: Purl.

Row 3: K9, ssk, yo, k1, yo, k2tog, k9.

Row 5: K1, ssk, k6, ssk, yo, k1, yo, k2tog, k6, k2tog, k1—21 sts.

Row 7 and all odd-numbered rows through 15: Cont in patt, dec 1 st at beg and end of row as in Row 5— 11 sts after Row 15.

Row 16: Purl, then cable CO 5 sts—16 sts.

Row 17: K8, ssk, yo, k1, yo, k2tog, k3, cable CO 5 more sts—21 sts.

Row 19 and all odd-numbered rows through 29: Cont in patt, dec 1 st at beg and end of row as before—9 sts after Row 29.

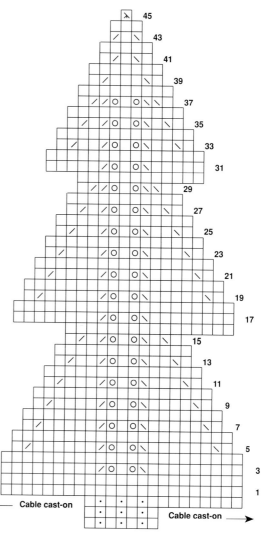

Row 30: Purl, then cable CO 3 sts—12 sts.

Row 31: K5, ssk, yo, k1, yo, k2tog, k2, cable CO 3 more sts—15 sts.

Rows 33, 35, and 37: Cont in patt, dec 1 st at beg and end of row as before—9 sts after Row 37.

Row 39: K1, ssk, k3, k2tog, k1—7 sts.

Row 41: K1, ssk, k1, k2tog, k1—5 sts.

Row 43: Ssk, k1, k2tog—3 sts.

Row 45: Sl 1, k2tog, psso—1 st. Fasten off.

Medium: CO 7 sts. Work k1, p1 rib until piece measures 1" (2.5 cm).

Rows 1–29: Work as for large version—9 sts.

Rows 30–37: Work as for Rows 38–45 of large version.

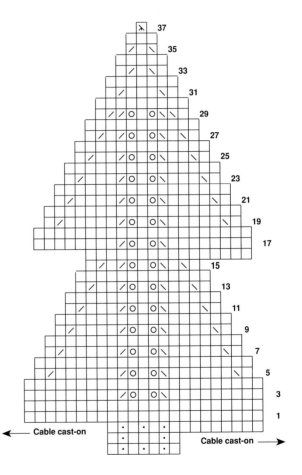

Appliqué

Small: CO 7 sts. Work k1, p1 rib until piece measures 1" (2.5 cm).
Rows 1–16: Work as for large version.
Row 17: K1, ssk, k5, k2tog, k1.
Rows 18–25: Work as for Rows 38–45 of large version.

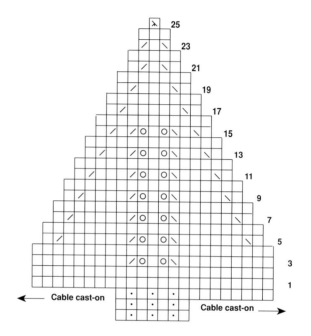

Seed-Stitch Tree
(Worked from the top down.)

Top: CO 1 st.
Set-up row: Knit.
Row 1: (K1, p1, k1) in same st—3 sts.
Row 2: K1, p1, k1.
Row 3: K1f&b, p1, k1f&b— 5 sts.
Row 4: [P1, k1] 2 times, p1.
Row 5: K1f&b, k1, p1, k1, k1f&b—7 sts.

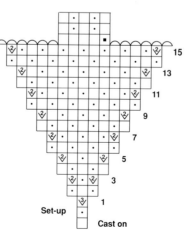

Row 6: K1, [p1, k1] 3 times.

Rows 7–14: Cont inc 1 st each end of needle every other row—15 sts after Row 14. Knit 1 row.
BO 5 sts, k4, BO 5 sts, cut yarn and draw through rem st. Fasten off—5 sts rem.

Trunk: Work in k1, p1 rib for 1¼" (3.2 cm). BO all sts.

Garter-Stitch Tree

(Worked from the top down.)

Top: CO 1 st. Knit every row, working k1f&b inc at beg of every row until there are 15 sts. BO 5 sts, k4, BO 5 sts, cut yarn and draw through rem st.

Trunk: Work k1, p1 rib for 1¼" (3.2 cm). BO all sts.

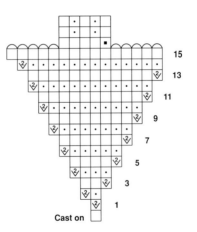

Faux Fur Tree

(Worked from the top down.)

The loops on this tree resemble fur. Cut them for an even more furry look.

Faux Fur Stitch: (multiple of 2 sts + 1; worked on WS) K1, *Make loop: insert needle in st, wrap yarn over needle kwise then over one finger of left hand, then over needle again (2 loops on needle). Draw both loops on needle through the st. Insert left needle through the front of the loops and knit them tog tbl rep from *.

Trunk: CO 5 sts. Knit every row for 1" (2.5 cm), ending with a WS row. Cut yarn, leave sts on needle.

Top: On same needle, join new yarn then use the cable method (page 259) to CO 10 sts, turn. Knit the CO sts, then knit rem sts, cable CO 10 more sts—25 sts.

Row 1: (WS) Work Faux Fur st.

Rows 2 and 4: Knit.

Row 3: Ssk, work Faux Fur st to last 2 sts, k2tog—23 sts.

Rep Rows 1–4 until 3 sts rem. Sl 1, k2tog, psso—1 st. Fasten off.

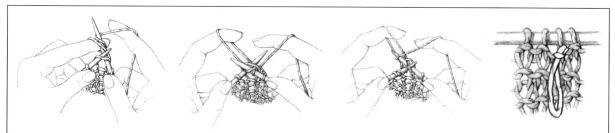

Make loop: *Insert needle in st, wrap yarn over needle kwise, then wrap yarn over one finger (or more for a larger loop) of left hand, then over needle again (2 loops on needle).*

Draw both loops on needle through the st.

Insert left needle through the front of the loops and knit them tog through back loops.

Completed loop as seen from right side of work.

Potted Tree

Pot: CO 7 sts. Work in St st for 1" (2.5 cm). At end of last WS row, use the cable method (page 259) to CO 3 sts, k10, turn, cable CO 3 more sts—13 sts. Work in St st for 6 rows. BO all sts. Allow pot top to roll and sew in place.

Trunk: Pick up and knit 5 center sts of pot, ½" (1.3 cm) down from pot top. Work k1, p1 rib for 1" (2.5 cm), and then on same needle, cable CO 5 sts—10 sts.

Tree:

Row 1: K10, turn, cable CO 5 more sts—15 sts.

Row 2 and all even-numbered rows except 10 and 20: Purl.

Row 3: K1, k2tog, k9, ssk, k1—13 sts.

Rows 5 and 13: K1, k2tog, k7, ssk, k1—11 sts.

Rows 7 and 15: K1, k2tog, k5, ssk, k1—9 sts.

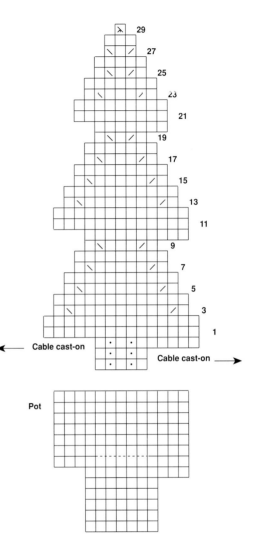

Cable cast-on

Cable cast-on

Pot

- - - - - - - - Pick up for trunk along these sts.

Rows 9 and 17: K1, k2tog, k3, ssk, k1—7 sts.

Row 10: Purl, then cable CO 3 sts—10 sts.

Row 11: K10, cable CO 3 more sts—13 sts.

Row 19: K1, k2tog, k1, ssk, k1—5 sts.

Row 20: Purl, then cable CO 2 sts—7 sts.

Row 21: K7, cable CO 2 more sts—9 sts.

Row 23: K1, k2tog, k3, ssk, k1—7 sts.

Row 25: K1, k2tog, k1, ssk, k1—5 sts.

Row 27: K2tog, k1, ssk—3 sts.

Row 29: Sl 1, k2tog, psso. Fasten off. Sew overlapping portion of trunk to pot.

Patchwork Tree

Following instructions for the Garter Stitch Tree (page 61), work 9 triangles in varying colors and textures. Using the photograph as a guide, arrange triangles into tree shape and use whip st (page 206) to sew the edges tog. **Trunk:** CO 7 sts. Work garter stitch for 1" (2.5 cm). BO all sts. Use whip st to sew trunk in place.

Victoria's Tree

Top: CO 46 sts.

Row 1: (RS) [K4, p2] 3 times, k4, p2, k4, [p2, k4] 3 times.

Rows 2 and 4: Knit the knits and purl the purls.

Row 3: [2/2LC, p2] 3 times, place 2 sts onto cn and hold in
    front, k2, k1 from cn, ssk (rem st on cn with first purl st), sl
    next (p1) st to right needle, place next 2 sts onto cn and
    hold in back, sl st back to left needle, k2tog (first knit st

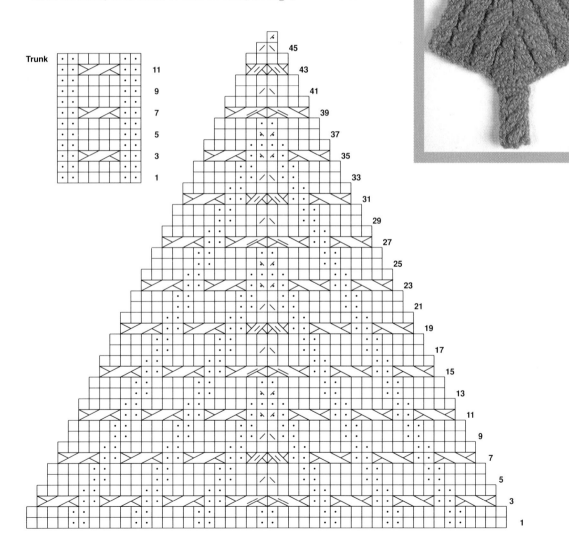

Trunk

and purl st), k1, k2 from cn, [p2, 2/2RC] 3 times—44 sts.

Cont in this manner, turning cables every 4th row and dec 1 st in patt each side of center front as shown on chart every 2nd row until 2 sts rem. P2tog—1 st. Fasten off.

Trunk: CO 8 sts.

Row 1: P2, k4, p2.

Rows 2 and 4: Knit the knits and purl the purls.

Row 3: P2, 2/2RC, p2.

Rows 5–12: Rep Rows 1–4 two more times. BO all sts. Sew trunk to center bottom of tree.

Bobble Tree

Bobble: CO 1 st.

Row 1: ([K1f&b] 2 times, k1) in same st—5 sts.

Rows 2 and 4: Purl.

Row 3: Knit.

Row 5: K2tog, k1, k2tog—3 sts.

Row 6: P3tog—1 st. Fasten off.

Make 21 bobbles. Work 4-st knit cord (page 149) for 2" (5 cm). Arrange bobbles in triangular shape and sew in place; sew knit cord to base for trunk.

Apple Tree

Trunk: CO 11 sts. Work k1, p1 rib for 1" (2.5 cm), dec 1 st each end of needle on last row—9 sts.

Cont in patt for 1" (2.5 cm) more, dec 1 st each end of needle on last row—7 sts. Cont in patt for 1" (2.5 cm) more, end with a RS row.

Top:

Row 1: *K1, M1; rep from * to last st, k1—13 sts.

Row 2: Knit.

Rows 3–6: Rep Rows 1–2 two more times—49 sts after Row 6.

Rows 7–18: Work garter st—6 ridges after Row 18.

Rows 19–38: Cont in garter st, dec 1 st (k2tog) at beg of every row—30 sts after Row 37.

Row 38: Ssk, BO rem sts.

With WS facing, BO all sts. Work French knots (page 203) for apples.

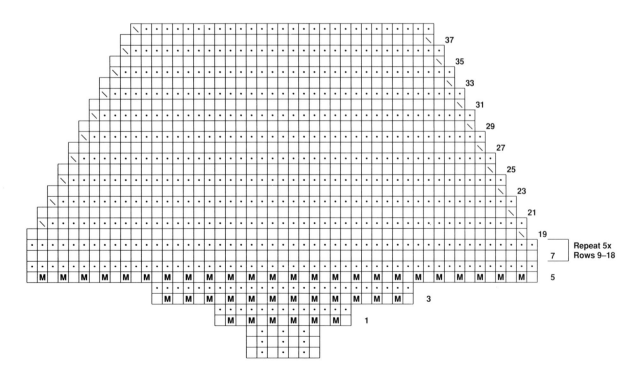

Happy Tree

Trunk: CO 5 sts. Work tube st (page 151) for 6 rows. On same needle and using the cable method (page 259), CO 6 sts—11 sts.

Row 1: (RS) K11, cable CO 6 more sts—17 sts.

Row 2 and all even-numbered rows: Purl.

Row 3: Ssk, yo, ssk, k9, k2tog, yo, k2tog—15 sts.

Row 5: Ssk, yo, ssk, k7, k2tog, yo, k2tog—13 sts.

Row 7: Ssk, yo, ssk, k5, k2tog, yo, k2tog—11 sts.

Row 9: Ssk, yo, ssk, k3, k2tog, yo, k2tog—9 sts.

Row 11: Ssk, yo, ssk, k1, k2tog, yo, k2tog—7 sts.

Row 13: Ssk, yo, sl 2tog kwise, k1, p2sso, yo, k2tog—5 sts.

Row 15: Ssk, k1, k2tog—3 sts.

Row 17: Sl 2tog kwise, k1, p2sso—1 st. Fasten off.

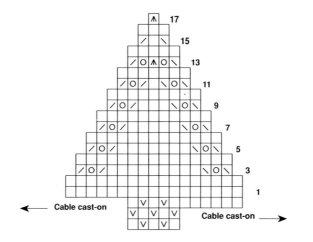

Tannenbaum

CO 7 sts. Work k1, p1 rib for 1" (2.5 cm), ending with a WS row. On the same needle and using the cable method (page 259), CO 8 sts—15 sts.

Row 1: (RS) K15, cable CO 8 more sts—23 sts.

Row 2 and all even-numbered rows except 16 and 30: Purl.

Row 3: K1, ssk, k8, yo, k1, yo, k8, k2tog, k1—23 sts.

Row 5: K1, ssk, k5, k2tog, yo, k3, yo, ssk, k5, k2tog, k1—21 sts.

Row 7: K1, ssk, k3, k2tog, yo, k5, yo, ssk, k3, k2tog, k1—19 sts.

Row 9: K1, ssk, k1, k2tog, yo, k7, yo, ssk, k1, k2tog, k1—17 sts.

Row 11: K1, ssk, k3, k2tog, yo, k1, yo, ssk, k3, k2tog, k1—15 sts.

Row 13: K1, ssk, k1, k2tog, yo, k3, yo, ssk, k1, k2tog, k1—13 sts.

Row 15: K1, sl 1, k2tog, psso, yo, k5, yo, k3tog, k1, cable CO 5 sts—16 sts.

Row 16: P16, cable CO 5 sts—21 sts.

Row 17: K1, ssk, k4, yo, k7, yo, k4, k2tog, k1.

Row 19: K1, ssk, k5, k2tog, yo, k1, yo, ssk, k5, k2tog, k1—19 sts.

Row 21: K1, ssk, k3, k2tog, yo, k3, yo, ssk, k3, k2tog, k1—17 sts.

Row 23: K1, ssk, k1, k2tog, yo, k5, yo, ssk, k1, k2tog, k1—15 sts.

Row 25: K1, sl 1, k2tog, psso, yo, k7, yo, k3tog, k1—13 sts.

Row 27: K1, ssk, k1, k2tog, yo, k1, yo, ssk, k1, k2tog, k1—11 sts.

Row 29: Ssk, k2tog, yo, k3, yo, ssk, k2tog, cable CO 3 sts—12 sts.

Row 30: P12, cable CO 3 sts—15 sts.

Row 31: K1, ssk, k2, yo, k5, yo, k2, k2tog, k1—15 sts.

Appliqué

Row 33: K1, sl 1, k2tog, psso, yo, k7, yo, k3tog, k1.

Row 35: K1, ssk, k1, k2tog, yo, k1, yo, ssk, k1, k2tog, k1—11 sts.

Row 37: K1, sl 1, k2tog, psso, yo, k3, yo, k3tog, k1—9 sts.

Row 39: K1, ssk, k3, k2tog, k1—7 sts.

Row 41: K1, ssk, k1, k2tog, k1—5 sts.

Row 43: Ssk, k1, k2tog—3 sts.

Row 45: Sl 1, k2tog, psso—1 st. Fasten off.

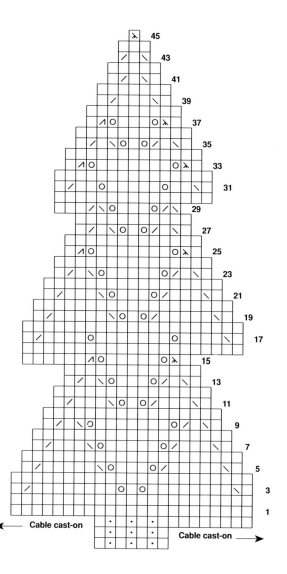

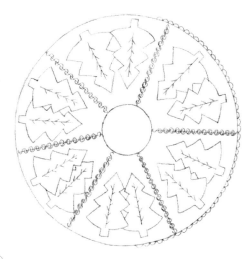

Christmas stocking and tree skirt with appliquéd pine trees, cable cord, and knit cord letters.

70

Scott's Pine

Trunk: CO 7 sts. Work k1, p1 rib for 1" (2.5 cm). On same needle and using the cable method (page 259), CO 8 sts—15 sts.

Row 1: (RS) K15, cable CO 8 more sts—23 sts.

Row 2 and all even-numbered rows except 14 and 28: Purl.

Row 3: Ssk, k3, yo, ssk, k9, k2tog, yo, k3, k2tog—21 sts.

Row 5: Ssk, k3, yo, ssk, k7, k2tog, yo, k3, k2tog—19 sts.

Row 7: Ssk, k3, yo, ssk, k5, k2tog, yo, k3, k2tog—17 sts.

Row 9: Ssk, k3, yo, ssk, k3, k2tog, yo, k3, k2tog—15 sts.

Row 11: Ssk, k3, yo, ssk, k1, k2tog, yo, k3, k2tog—13 sts.

Row 13: Ssk, k3, yo, sl 2tog kwise, k1, p2sso, yo, k3, k2tog—11 sts.

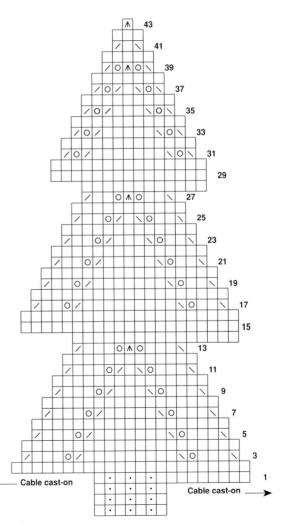

Row 14: P11, cable CO 5 sts—16 sts.

Row 15: K16, cable CO 5 sts—21 sts.

Row 17: Ssk, k2, yo, ssk, k9, k2tog, yo, k2, k2tog—19 sts.

Row 19: Ssk, k2, yo, ssk, k7, k2tog, yo, k2, k2tog—17 sts.

Row 21: Ssk, k2, yo, ssk, k5, k2tog, yo, k2, k2tog—15 sts.

Row 23: Ssk, k2, yo, ssk, k3, k2tog, yo, k2, k2tog—13 sts.

Row 25: Ssk, k2, yo, ssk, k1, k2tog, yo, k2, k2tog—11 sts.

Row 27: Ssk, k2, yo, sl 2tog kwise, k1, p2sso, yo, k2, k2tog—9 sts.

Row 28: P9, cable CO 3 sts—12 sts.

Row 29: K12, cable CO 3 sts—15 sts.

Row 31: Ssk, yo, ssk, k7, k2tog, yo, k2tog—13 sts.

Row 33: Ssk, yo, ssk, k5, k2tog, yo, k2tog—11 sts.

Row 35: Ssk, yo, ssk, k3, k2tog, yo, k2tog—9 sts.

Row 37: Ssk, yo, ssk, k1, k2tog, yo, k2tog—7 sts.

Row 39: Ssk, yo, sl 2tog kwise, k1, p2sso, yo, k2tog—5 sts.

Row 41: Ssk, k1, k2tog—3 sts.

Row 43: Sl 2tog kwise, k1, p2sso—1 st. Fasten off.

Cypress Tree

Trunk: CO 5 sts. Work tube st (page 151) for 1" (2.5 cm).

Top:

Row 1: (RS) K2, yo, k1, yo, k2—7 sts.

Row 2 and all even-numbered rows
except Rows 8 and 32: Purl.

Row 3: K3, yo, k1, yo, k3—9 sts.

Row 5: K4, yo, k1, yo, k4—11 sts.

Row 7: BO 3 sts, [k1, yo] 2 times,
k5—10 sts.

Row 8: BO 3 sts, p6—7 sts.

Rows 9–32: Rep Rows 3–8 four times.

Row 33: Ssk, k3, k2tog—5 sts.

Row 35: Ssk, k1, k2tog—3 sts.

Row 37: Sl 1, k2tog, psso. Fasten off.

Fruits and Vegetables

The following fruits and vegetables are three-dimensional motifs. The ones that are appliquéd are stuffed with fiberfill.

Berries, Grapes, or Cherries

Made from bobbles, these motifs can be used alone or in clusters. Make them bigger by working more stockinette-stitch rows between the shaping.

Variation 1 (shown on left)
CO 1 st.
Row 1: [K1f&b] 3 times—6 sts.
Rows 2 and 4: Purl.
Rows 3 and 5: Knit.
Row 6: [P2tog] 3 times—3 sts.
Row 7: Sl 1, k2tog, psso—1 st. Fasten off.

Variation 2 (shown on right above)
CO 1 st.
Row 1: ([K1f&b] 2 times, k1) in same st—5 sts.
Rows 2 and 4: Purl.
Row 3: Knit.
Row 5: Ssk, k1, k2tog—3 sts.
Row 6: P3tog—1 st. Fasten off.

Knot CO and BO tails tog and tuck into cherry. **Stem:** With crochet hook, attach stem yarn to cherry. Ch9 (page 262) for short stem; ch12 for long stem. Fasten off, leaving 3" (7.5-cm) tail for attaching.

Applique

Peas in a Pod

Pod: CO 1 st.

Row 1: [K1f&b] 3 times—6 sts.

Rows 2 and 4: Purl.

Row 3: K1, *[M1, k1] 5 times—11 sts. Work in St st until piece measures 3" (7.5 cm) from beg, end with a WS row.

Next row: K1, [k2tog] 5 times—6 sts. Do not turn. With left needle, pass 2nd, 3rd, 4th, 5th and 6th st over 1st st on right needle—1 st. Fasten off.

Peas (make 5) CO 1 st.

Row 1: ([K1f&b] 2 times, k1) in same st—5 sts.

Row 3: Knit.

Rows 2 and 4: Purl.

Row 5: Knit. Do not turn. With left needle, pass 2nd, 3rd, 4th, and 5th st over 1st st on right needle—1 st. Fasten off.

Attach peas by pulling CO and BO tails through to WS with crochet hook or tapestry needle. Knot securely on WS and bring tails back to RS and tuck into pea. With rev St st side of pea pod facing, sew peas into pod. Edges of pod will curl around peas.

Carrot

CO 1 st.

Row 1: [K1f&b] 3 times—6 sts.

Row 2: K1, [M1, k1] 5 times—11 sts.

Work in St st until piece measures 2" (5 cm) from beg, end with a WS row.

Row 3: K1, [k2tog] 5 times—6 sts.

Rows 4 and 6: Purl.

Row 5: [K2tog] 3 times—3 sts.

Row 7: K1, k2tog—2 sts.

Row 8: P2tog—1 st. Fasten off.

Stuff with scrap yarn. Sew seam.

Leaves: With crochet hook and St st side of carrot facing, join yarn to carrot top and work 3 to 4 chains (page 262), each 1½" to 2" (4 to 5 cm) in length.

Tomato

(Small tomato shown)

Small (Large) Tomato: With red, CO 9 (11) sts.

Row 1: Knit.

Row 2 and all even-numbered rows: Purl.

Row 3: K1, *[M1, k1] 8 (10) times—17 (21) sts. Work in St st until piece measures 2" (5 cm) from beg, end with a WS row.

Row 5: Knit, dec 8 (10) sts evenly spaced—9 (11) sts.

Row 7: Knit, dec 4 sts evenly spaced—5 (7) sts.

For small tomato only:

Row 9: Ssk, k1, k2tog—3 sts.

Row 11: Sl 1, k2tog, psso—1 st. Fasten off.

For large tomato only:

Row 9: Ssk, k3, k2tog—5 sts.

Row 11: Ssk, k1, k2tog—3 sts.

Row 13: Sl 1, k2tog, psso—1 st. Fasten off.

Small (Large) Leaf: CO 5 sts.

Row 1: Knit.

Row 2: BO 3 sts, p1—2 sts.

Row 3: K2, CO 3 sts—5 sts.

Row 4: Purl.

Rows 5–12 (20): Rep Rows 1–4 two (four) times.

Row 13 (21): Knit.

BO all sts. Gather straight edge tog tightly, sew to top of tomato. With crochet hook, join yarn and work 2" (5-cm) chain (page 262) for stem. Fasten off.

Eggplant

CO 11 sts.

Row 1: Knit.

Rows 2, 4, 6, 8, and 10: Purl.

Row 3: K1, *[M1, k1] 10 times—21 sts. Work even in St st until piece measures 2" (5 cm) from beg, end with a WS row.

Row 5: [K3, k2tog] 4 times, k1—17 sts.

Row 7: Knit.

Row 9: K2tog, [k3, k2tog] 3 times—13 sts.

Row 11: K1, [k2tog] 6 times—7 sts.

Row 12: P1, [p3tog] 3 times—4 sts. Do not turn. With left needle, pass 2nd, 3rd, and 4th st over 1st st on right needle—1 st. Fasten off.

Leaf: CO 5 sts.

Row 1: Knit.

Row 2: BO 3 sts, p1—2 sts.

Row 3: K2, CO 2 sts—5 sts.

Row 4: Purl.

Rows 5–12: Rep Rows 1–4 two times.

BO all sts. Sew to top of eggplant. *Stem:* With crochet hook, join yarn and work ¾" (2-cm) chain (page 262). Fasten off.

Two-Color Acorn

Variation 1: (Garter st top)

Base: CO 5 sts, leaving long tail for seaming.

Row 1: (RS) [K1f&b] 5 times—10 sts.

Rows 2, 4, 6, 8, and 10: Purl.

Rows 3, 5, 7, and 9: Knit.

Top: (Worked in CC)

Row 11: K1, [k1f&b] 8 times, k1—18 sts.

Rows 12–16: Knit.

Row 17: [K2tog] 9 times—9 sts.

Row 18: [K2tog] 4 times, k1—5 sts.

Cut yarn, leaving 12" (30.5-cm) tail. With tapestry needle, thread tail through rem sts on needle. Gather and fasten securely, but do not cut. With crochet hook, work same yarn in chain (page 262) about 2½" (6.5 cm) long. Stuff lightly. Gather CO edge with CO tail, sew seam, and fasten off.

Variation 2: (Rev St st top)

Base: CO and work through Row 9 as for variation 1.

Row 10: [p1, p1f&b] 9 times, p1—19 sts.

Top: (Worked in CC)

Rows 11 and 12: Knit.

Row 13–16: Work in rev St st.

Row 17: P1, [p2tog] 9 times—10 sts.

Row 18: [K2tog] 5 times—5 sts.

With tapestry needle, thread tail through rem sts on needle. Gather and fasten securely, but do not cut. With crochet hook, work same yarn in chain (page 262) about 2" (5 cm) long. Stuff lightly. Gather CO edge with CO tail, sew seam, and fasten off.

Miscellaneous Motifs

Package Ribbon and Bow

Make one strip for vertical ribbon, one for horizontal ribbon, one 9" (23 cm) long for bow, and one (using just 3 sts) 2" (5 cm) long for bow knot.

With MC, CO 7 sts or number required for desired width. Work in seed st for designated length. Sew one length centered vertically on background. Sew one length centered horizontally on same background. Sew two ends of 9" (23-cm) length tog and form into a bow. Wrap 2" (5-cm) length around center of bow and sew in place.

Shamrock

CO 3 sts. With separate ball of yarn, CO 3 more sts on same
   needle—6 sts total.

Row 1: (RS) *[K1, M1] 2 times, k1; rep from * on second set
   of sts—5 sts each set.

Row 2: Purl.

Row 3: *K1, M1, k3, M1, k1; rep from * on second set of sts—
   7 sts each set.

Row 4: Join the two sets as follows: P6, p2tog, p6—13 sts.

Row 5: *K1, M1, k11, M1, k1—15 sts.

Rows 6, 8, 10, 12, and 14: Purl.

Row 7: K6, sl 2tog kwise, k1, p2sso, k6—13 sts.

Row 9: K5, sl 2tog kwise, k1, p2sso, k5—11 sts.

Row 11: Ssk, k2, sl 2tog kwise, k2, p2sso, k2, k2tog—7 sts.

Row 13: Ssk, sl 2tog kwise, k1, p2sso, k2tog—3 sts.

Row 15: P3tog. Place rem st on holder.

Rep Rows 1–15 twice, leaving last st of last petal on needle.

Row 16: Using dpn, knit st on needle, then knit the 2 sts from holder onto same needle—3 sts.

   Work knit cord (page 149) for 4" (10 cm). BO all sts.

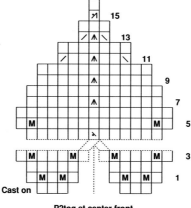

Cast on

P2tog at center front.

Circle

The basic circle can be adapted to your yarn and the size you want by simply casting on and increasing more or fewer stitches than the pattern calls for. The sample is worked in garter st.

CO 10 sts. Knit 2 rows. Inc 1 st (k1f&b) each end of every other row until there are 20 sts. Work even for 1½" (3.8 cm), ending with a WS row. *Next row:* Ssk, k16, k2tog. Cont to dec in this manner every other RS row until there are 10 sts. BO all sts.

Block

Cast on the number of stitches needed for the desired width of block and work any stitch until height measures same as width.

Spade

Left base: CO 5 sts.
Row 1: (RS) K1, M1, k3, M1, k1—7 sts.
Rows 2, 4, and 6: Purl.
Row 3: K1, M1, k5, M1, k1—9 sts.
Row 5: K1, M1, k7, M1, k1—11 sts.
Row 7: Knit.
Row 8: Purl. Cut yarn, leave sts on needle.
Stem: On same needle, CO 9 sts.
Row 1: K1, ssk, k3, k2tog, k1—7 sts.
Rows 2 and 4: Purl.
Row 3: Knit.
Row 5: K1, ssk, k1, k2tog, k1—5 sts.
Rows 6–14: Work in St st. Cut yarn, leave sts on needle.
Right base: On same needle, CO 5 sts.

Appliqué

Row 1: (RS) K1, M1, k3, M1, k1—7 sts.

Rows 2, 4, and 6: Purl.

Row 3: K1, M1, k5, M1, k1—9 sts.

Row 5: K1, M1, k7, M1, k1—11 sts.

Row 7: Knit.

Row 8: Purl—27 sts total on needle.

Row 9: (Joining row) K10, k2tog (last st of right base with first st of stem), k3, k2tog (last st of stem with first st of left base), k10—25 sts.

Row 10: Purl.

Rows 11–19: Work in St st.

Row 21 and all odd numbered rows through 39:
  K1, ssk, knit to last 3 sts, k2tog, k1—2 sts dec'd;
  5 sts rem after Row 39.

Row 20 and all even-numbered rows: Purl.

Row 41: Ssk, k1, k2tog—3 sts.

Row 43: P3tog—1 st.

Fasten off.

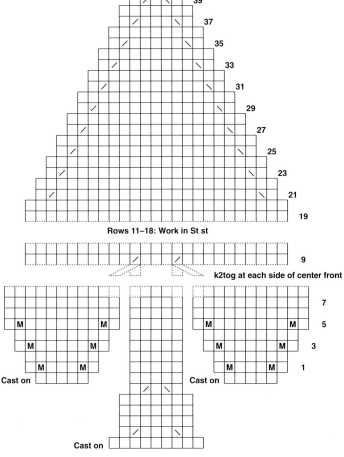

80

Diamond

CO 3 sts.

Row 1: (RS) Knit.

Row 2 and all even-numbered rows except 42: Purl.

Row 3: [K1, M1] 2 times, k1—5 sts.

Row 5: K1, M1, k3, M1, k1—7 sts.

Row 7: K1, M1, k5, M1, k1—9 sts.

Rows 9–22: Cont to inc 2 sts in this manner every other row—23 sts.

Row 23: K1, ssk, knit to last 3 sts, k2tog, k1.

Rows 25–39: Cont to dec 2 sts in this manner every other row until 5 sts rem.

Row 41: Ssk, k1, k2tog—3 sts.

Row 42: P3tog—1 st. Fasten off.

Heart

Top: CO 3 sts. With separate ball of yarn, CO 3 more sts on same needle—6 sts total.

Row 1: (RS) *[K1, M1] 2 times, k1; rep from * on second set of sts—5 sts each set.

Row 2 and all even-numbered rows: Purl.

Row 3: *K1, M1, k3, M1, k1; rep from * over second set of sts—7 sts each set.

Rows 5–8: Cont working incs in this manner until there are 11 sts each set.

Body:

Row 9: (Joining row) K1, M1, k9, k2tog, k9, M1, k1—23 sts. Cut second yarn.

Rows 10–12: Work even in St st.

Rows 13–30: K1, ssk, knit to last 3 sts, k2tog, k1—2 sts dec'd. Cont in St st, dec 2 sts every other row in this manner until 5 sts rem, end with a WS row.

Row 31: K1, sl 1, k2tog, psso, k1—3 sts.

Row 32: Purl.

Row 33: Sl 1, k2tog, psso—1 st. Fasten off.

Appliqué

Club

CO 5 sts.

Row 1: (RS) [K1, M1] 4 times, k1—9 sts.

Row 2 and all even-numbered rows through 16: Purl.

Row 3: [K1, M1] 8 times, k1—17 sts.

Rows 5 and 7: Knit.

Row 9: K7, sl 2 sts tog kwise, k1, p2sso, k7—15 sts.

Row 11: K6, sl 2 sts tog kwise, k1, p2sso, k6—
    13 sts.

Row 13: K5, sl 2 sts tog kwise, k1, p2sso, k5—
    11 sts.

Row 15: K4, sl 2 sts tog kwise, k1, p2sso, k4—9 sts.

Row 17: K3, sl 2 sts tog kwise, k1, p2sso, k3—7 sts.

Row 18: Purl. Leave sts on needle.

With same needle and new yarn, rep Rows 1–18 two more times—21 sts.

Row 19: K6, k2tog, k5, k2tog, k6—19 sts.

Rows 20 and 22: Purl.

Row 21: K1, [k2tog] 9 times—10 sts.

Row 23: [K2tog] 5 times—5 sts.

Rows 24–32: Work in St st.

Row 33: [K1, M1] 2 times, k1—9 sts.

Row 34: Purl.

Row 35: Knit.

Row 36: Purl.

BO all sts in knit.

Reverse stockinette stitch pullover with appliquéd hearts, leaves, knit cord, and a leaf edging.

82

Borders and Edgings

Ribs

Knitters around the world have traditionally edged sweaters with basic 1x1 or 2x2 ribs, the theory being that the elasticity of ribs provides a snug fit that helps retain body heat. For practicality and design, these standard rib edges are still widely used. However, with a little imagination, these ribs can be as decorative as they are practical.

1x1 Basic Rib

Note: The sample shows a 1x1 rib that turns into St st. It is embellished with a 4-st knit cord (page 149).

Worked on an even number of sts
Row 1: (RS) *K1, p1; rep from *.
Rep Row 1 for desired length.

Worked on an odd number of sts
Row 1: (RS) *K1, p1; rep from *, end k1.
Row 2: *P1, k1; rep from *, end p1.
Rep Rows 1 and 2 for desired length.

1x1 Horizontal Rib

Work desired depth of ribbing in a vertical fashion for length needed. BO all sts. Turn piece so that long edge is oriented horizontally. Pick up and knit sts along the long edge and work as desired.

1x1 Striped Rib

With A, CO an even number of sts.

Row 1: *K1, p1; rep from *.

Rep Row 1 for desired length, end with a WS row. Change to B, and knit 1 row. Rep Row 1 for desired length, end with a WS row. Each time a new color is added, knit 1 row, then rep Row 1 for desired length.

1x1 Broken Rib

CO an even number of sts.

Row 1: *K1, p1; rep from *.

Rep Row 1 for 1" (2.5 cm), end with a WS row.

Next row: *P1, k1; rep from *.

Rep this row for 1" (2.5 cm), end with a WS row.

Rep from Row 1 for desired length.

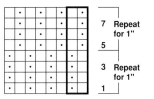

1x1 Eyelet Rib

CO an even number of sts.

Rows 1 and 2: *K1, p1; rep from *.

Rep Rows 1 and 2 for 1" (2.5 cm) or desired length, end with a WS row.

Row 3: K1, *yo, k2tog; rep from *, end k1.

Rows 4 and 5: *P1, k1; rep from *.

Rep Rows 4 and 5 for desired length. Thread ribbon through eyelets and tie into bow, if desired.

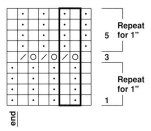

1x1 Two-Color Rib

With A, CO an odd number of sts. Join B.

Row 1: (RS) *K1 with A, k1 with B; rep from *, end k1 with A.

Row 2: P1 with A, *k1 with B, p1 with A; rep from *.

Row 3: *K1 with A, p1 with B; rep from *, end k1 with A.

Rep Rows 2 and 3 for desired length.

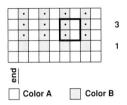

☐ Color A   ▨ Color B

1x1 Layered Rib

CO and work 1x1 Rib (page 83) for 2" (5 cm). Leave sts on needle. Set aside. With another ball of yarn and spare needle, CO and work 1x1 Rib for 1" (2.5 cm). Leave sts on needle. Place shorter rib in front of longer rib. With a third needle, k2tog (1 st from front needle tog with 1 st from back needle).

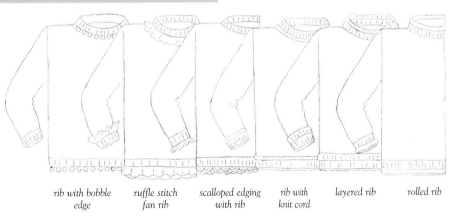

| rib with bobble edge | ruffle stitch fan rib | scalloped edging with rib | rib with knit cord | layered rib | rolled rib |

Decorative ribs can greatly enhance the look of a simple sweater.
Shown here are six of the ideas presented in this chapter.

1x1 Rolled Rib

(multiple of 2 sts)

Cast-On Version: CO and work St st for desired length of roll. Then work 1x1 Rib (page 83) for desired length.

Bind-Off Version: Work 1x1 Rib (page 83) for desired length. Then work St st for desired length of roll. BO all sts.

1x1 Fence Rib

(multiple of 12 sts + 5)

Either side of this pattern may be used for the right side.

Row 1: *K1, p1; rep from *, end k1.

Row 2: Knit the knits and purl the purls.

Rep Rows 1 and 2 for desired length.

Row 3: *[K1, p1] 2 times, k1, p7; rep from *, end [k1, p1] 2 times, k1.

Row 4: Knit the knits and purl the purls.

Rep Rows 3 and 4 for desired length.

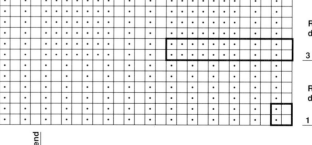

Repeat for desired length

3

Repeat for desired length

1

end

1x1 Graduated Rib

(multiple of 12 sts + 3)

Row 1: K1, *p1, k1; rep from *.

Row 2: Knit the knits and purl the purls.

Rep Rows 1 and 2 for 1" (2.5 cm) or desired length, end with Row 1.

Inc Row: (WS) P2, *M1, rib 11 as established, M1, p1; rep from *, end p2—mult of 14 sts + 3.

Row 3: K2, *1/1LC, rib 9, 1/1RC, k1; rep from *, end last rep k2.

Rows 4, 6, 8, and 10: Knit the knits and purl the purls.

Row 5: K3, *1/1LCP, rib 7, 1/1RCP, k3; rep from *.

Row 7: K2, *1/1LC, 1/1LCP, rib 5, 1/1RCP, 1/1RC, k1; rep from *, end last rep k2.

Row 9: K3, *[1/1LCP] 2 times, rib 3, [1/1RCP] 2 times, k3; rep from *.

Row 11: K2, *1/1LC, [1/1LCP] 2 times, p1, [1/1RCP] 2 times, 1/1RC, k1; rep from *, end last rep k2.

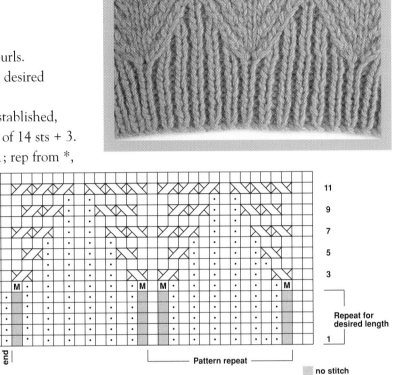

1x1 Ruffle Stitch Fan Rib

This edging can be picked up and worked directly onto a piece or it can be worked separately and then sewn onto a finished piece.

CO or pick up an odd number of sts.

Work 1x1 Rib for 1½" (3.8 cm).

Row 1: K1, *p1, M1 pwise, k1; rep from *.

Row 2 and all even-numbered rows: Knit the knits and purl the purls.

Row 3: K1, *p2, M1 pwise, k1; rep from *.

Row 5: K1, *p3, M1, k1; rep from *.
Row 7: K1, *p4, M1, k1; rep from *.
Row 9: K1, *p5, M1, k1; rep from *.
For a contrasting edge, BO in knit with CC.

Note: Without the ribbing, Rows 1–10 of this edging can be worked directly onto a piece, or the edging can be worked separately and then sewn to a finished piece.

1x1 and Spiral Rib

(multiple of 13 sts + 7)

Row 1: (RS) P1, [k1, p1] 3 times, *[k2tog, then knit first st again] 3 times, [p1, k1] 3 times, p1; rep from *.
Rows 2 and 4: Knit the knits and purl the purls.
Row 3: [P1, k1] 4 times, *[k2tog, then knit first st again] 2 times, [k1, p1] 4 times; rep from *.
Rep Rows 1–4 for desired length.

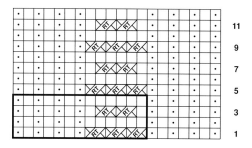

1x1 Woven Diamond Rib

(multiple of 19 sts + 3)

Work all knit sts through back loop on RS; work all purl sts through back loop on WS. Work all cables in reverse on the back, i.e., 1/1RC is worked as 2 knit sts on the front of work and as 2 purl sts on back of work. The direction (either right or left) that the sts move remains the same.
Rows 1, 3, 5, 19, 21, and 23: (RS) P1, [k1b] 3 times, *[p1, k1b] 2 times, p2, k2tog then knit the first st again, p2, [k1b, p1] 2 times, [k1b] 5 times; rep from *, end last rep [k1b] 3 times, p1.
Rows 2, 4, 6, 18, 20, and 22: Knit the knits; purl the purls through the back loops.

Row 7: P1, [k1b] 3 times, *p1, k1b, p1, [1/1LCP, 1/1RCP] 2 times, p1, k1b, p1, [k1b] 5 times; rep from *, end last rep [k1b] 3 times, p1.

Row 8: K1, [p1b] 3 times, *k1, p1b, k2, [1/1LC, k2] 2 times, p1b, k1, [p1b] 2 times; rep from *, end last rep [p1b] 3 times, k1.

Rows 9 and 13: P1, [k1b] 3 times, *p1, [1/1LCP, 1/1RCP] 3 times, p1, [k1b] 5 times; rep from *, end last rep [k1b] 3 times, p1.

Rows 10 and 14: K1, [p1b] 3 times, *[k2, 1/1RC] 3 times, k2, [p1b] 5 times; rep from *, end last rep [p1b] 3 times, k1.

Rows 11 and 15: P1, [k1b] 3 times, *p1, [1/1RCP, 1/1LCP] 3 times, p1, [k1b] 5 times; rep from *, end last rep [k1b] 3 times, p1.

Row 12: K1, [p1b] 3 times, *k1, p1, [k2, 1/1LCP] 2 times, k2, p1, k1, [p1] 5 times; rep from *, end last rep [p1b] 3 times, k1.

Row 16: K1, [p1b] 3 times, *k1, p1b, [k2, 1/1LCP] 2 times, k2, p1b, k1 [p1b] 5 times; rep from *, end last rep [p1b] 3 times, k1.

Row 17: P1, [k1b] 3 times, *p1, k1b, p1, [1/1RCP, 1/1LCP] 2 times, p1, k1b, p1, [k1b] 5 times; rep from *, end last rep [k1b] 3 times, p1.

Row 24: Rep Row 2.

BO in patt on Row 24 or rep Rows 7–24 for desired length.

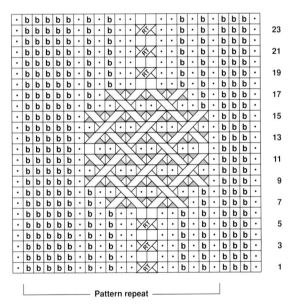

Pattern repeat

1x1 Colored Woven Diamond Rib

(multiple of 19 sts + 3)

Note: With appropriate color, work all knit sts through back loop on RS; work all purl sts through back loop on WS.

With MC, CO desired number of sts.

Foundation row: (WS) (K1, [p1b] 3 times, k1) with MC, *p1b with A, k1 with MC, p1b with B, k2 with MC, p2b with C, k2 with MC, p1b with B, k1 with MC, p1b with A, (k1, [p1b] 5 times, k1) with MC; rep from *, end last rep [p1b] 3 times, k1.

With appropriate colors, work Rows 1–24 of 1x1 Woven Diamond (page 88).

1x1 Rib with Bobbles

(multiple of 4 sts + 3)

Bobble (MB): ([p1, k1] 2 times) in same st— 4 sts, then sl 2nd, 3rd, and 4th sts over 1st st.

Cast-On Version: CO desired number of sts.

Rows 1 and 5: (RS) P1, *k1, p1; rep from *.

Rows 2, 4, and 6: *K1, p1; rep from *, end k1.

Row 3: P1, *k1, p1, MB, p1; rep from *.

Rep Rows 1–6 for desired length, then work 1x1 Rib for desired length.

Bind-Off Version: Work as for CO version, working 1x1 Rib for desired length followed by Rows 1–6.

1x1 Vertical Bobble Rib

(multiple of 6 sts + 5)

Bobble (MB): ([P1, k1] 2 times) in same st—4 sts, then sl 2nd, 3rd, and 4th sts over 1st st.

Rows 1 and 3: (RS) *P1, k1; rep from *, end p1.

Row 2: K1, *[p1, k1] 2 times, MB, k1; rep from *, end [p1, k1] 2 times.

Row 4: Knit the knits and purl the purls.

Rep Rows 1–4 for desired length.

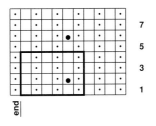

1x1 Two-Color Vertical Bobble Rib

(multiple of 6 sts + 5)

Bobble (MB): ([P1, k1] 2 times) in same st—4 sts, then sl 2nd, 3rd, and 4th sts over 1st st.

With A, CO desired number of sts.

Rows 1 and 3: (RS) [P1, k1] 2 times with A, *(p1, k1, p1) with B, (k1, p1, k1) with A; rep from *, end last rep p1 with A.

Row 2: K1, *(p1, k1, p1) with A, (k1, MB, k1) with B; rep from *, end last rep [p1, k1] 2 times with A.

Row 4: Knit the knits and purl the purls in established colors.

Rep Rows 1–4 for desired length.

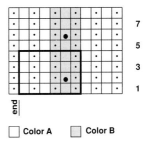

□ Color A   ▨ Color B

1x1 Rib and Cable Combination

(multiple of 9 sts + 5)

Row 1: (RS) *[P1, k1] 2 times, p1, k4; rep from *,
  end p1, [k1, p1] 2 times.
Rows 2 and 4: Knit the knits and purl the purls.
Row 3: *[P1, k1] 2 times, p1, *2/2RC; rep from *,
  end p1, [k1, p1] 2 times.
Rep Rows 1–4 for desired length.

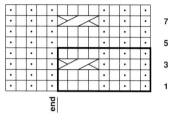

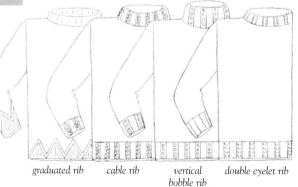

2x2 Basic Rib

(multiple of 4 sts + 2)

Row 1: (RS) *K2, p2; rep from *, end k2.
Row 2: P2, *k2, p2; rep from *.
Rep Rows 1 and 2 for desired length.

graduated rib   cable rib   vertical   double eyelet rib
                                          bobble rib

*Next time your pattern calls for a 2 × 2 rib, try one of these
variations for a more interesting look.*

2x2 Striped Rib

(multiple of 4 sts + 2)

With A, CO desired number of sts.
Rows 1 and 3: (RS) *K2, p2; rep from *, end k2.
Rows 2 and 4: P2, *k2, p2; rep from *.
Row 5: Change to B, knit.
Rows 6 and 8: P2, *k2, p2; rep from *.
Row 7: *K2, p2; rep from *, end k2.
Rep Rows 5–8 for each new color.

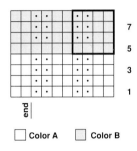

☐ Color A   ☐ Color B

2x2 Rolled Rib

(multiple of 4 sts + 2)

Cast-On Version: (shown) CO and work St st for desired length of roll. Then work 2x2 Basic Rib (page 92) for desired length.

Bind-Off Version: Work 2x2 Basic Rib (page 92) for desired length. Then work St st for desired length of roll. BO all sts.

2x2 Two-Color Rib

(multiple of 4 sts + 2)

With A, CO desired number of sts.

Row 1: (RS) *K2 with A, k2 with B; rep from *, end k2 with A.

Row 2: P2 with A, *k2 with B, p2 with A; rep from *.

Row 3: *K2 with A, p2 with B; rep from *, end k2 with A.

Rep Rows 2 and 3 for desired length.

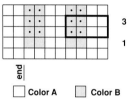

☐ Color A   ▦ Color B

2x2 Broken Basketweave Rib

(multiple of 4 sts + 2)

Rows 1 and 3: (RS) *K2, p2; rep from *, end k2.

Rows 2, 4, 6, and 8: and all even-numbered rows: Knit the knits and purl the purls.

Rows 5 and 7: *P2, k2; rep from *, end p2.

Rep Rows 1–8 for desired length.

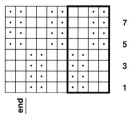

Eyelet Rib with Bobbles

(multiple of 5 sts + 2)

Bobble (MB): ([k1, p1] 2 times, k1) in same st, turn, k5, turn, p5, pass 2nd, 3rd, 4th, and 5th st over 1st st.

Row 1: P2, *k1, yo, ssk, p2; rep from *.

Rows 2 and 4: *K2, p3; rep from *.

Row 3: P2, *k2tog, yo, p2; rep from *.

Rep Rows 1–4 for desired length. With RS facing, pick up and knit 1 st in each st along CO edge.

Row 1: P3, *MB, p4; rep from *, end p3.

Row 2: BO all sts as to knit.

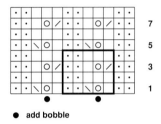

● add bobble

Double Eyelet Rib

(multiple of 7 sts + 2)

Note: Sample shows two 3-st knit cords (page 149) sewn to CO edge.

Row 1: (RS) P2, *k5, p2; rep from *.

Rows 2 and 4: Knit the knits and purl the purls.

Row 3: P2, *k2tog, yo, k1, yo, ssk, p2; rep from *.

Rep Rows 1–4 for desired length.

Canada Lace

(multiple of 11 sts + 6)

Row 1: (RS) P2, 1/1LC, p2, *yo, ssk, k1, k2tog, yo, p2, 1/1LC, p2; rep from *.

Rows 2 and 4: *K2, p2, k2, p5; rep from*, end k2, p2, k2.

Row 3: P2, 1/1LC, p2, *k1, yo, sl 1 kwise, k2tog, psso, yo, k1, p2, 1/1LC, p2; rep from *.

Rep Rows 1–4 for desired length.

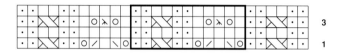

Rose's Rib with Picot

(multiple of 11 sts + 4)

Rows 1 and 5: (RS) K1, yo, p2tog, k1, *p1, k2, yo, ssk, k1, p1, k1, yo, p2tog, k1; rep from *.

Rows 2, 4, 6, and 8: *K1, yo, p2tog, k2, p5, k1; rep from *, end k1, yo, p2tog, p1.

Row 3: K1, yo, p2tog, k1, *p1, k1, yo, sl 1 kwise, k2tog, psso, yo, k1, p1, k1, yo, p2tog, k1; rep from *.

Row 7: K1, yo, p2tog, k1, *p1, k5, p1, k1, yo, p2tog, k1; rep from *.

Rep Rows 1–8 for desired length.

Picot edge: Using the backward loop method (page 260), CO 4 sts. *BO 3 sts, CO 3 sts; rep from * for desired length. BO all sts. Sew in place to rib CO edge.

Chevron Lace Rib with Rolled Edge

(multiple of 7 sts + 2)

CO desired number of sts. Work St st for 1" (2.5 cm).

Row 1: (RS) K1, *k1, k2tog, yo, k1, yo, ssk, k1; rep from *, end last rep k2.

Rows 2 and 4: Purl.

Row 3: K1, *k2tog, yo, k3, yo, ssk; rep from *, end k1.

Rep Rows 1–4 for desired length.

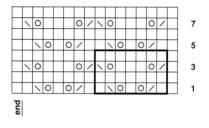

Lace Column Rib

(multiple of 6 sts + 5)

Row 1: (RS) Knit.

Rows 2 and 4: Purl.

Row 3: K1, *yo, sl 1 kwise, k2tog, psso, yo, k3; rep from *, end yo, sl 1 kwise, k2tog, psso, yo, k1.

Rep Rows 1–4 for desired length.

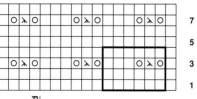

Pearled Diamond Rib

(multiple of 9 sts + 2)

Row 1: P2, *k2tog, [k1, yo] 2 times, k1, ssk, p2;
  rep from *.

Rows 2, 4, 6, and 8: Knit the knits and purl the
  purls.

Row 3: P2, *k2tog, yo, k3, yo, ssk, p2; rep from *.

Row 5: P2, *k1, yo, ssk, k1, k2tog, yo, k1, p2; rep
  from *.

Row 7: P2, *k2, yo, sl 1 kwise, k2tog, psso, yo, k2,
  p2; rep from *.

Rep Rows 1–8 for desired length.

■ Sew pearl

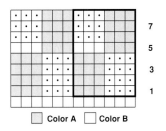

☐ Color A ☐ Color B

3x3 Two-Color Checked Rib

(multiple of 6 sts)

With B, CO desired number of sts.

Rows 1 and 3: (RS) *P3 with B, k3 with A; rep
  from *.

Row 2, 4, 6, and 8: Knit the knits and purl the
  purls with established colors.

Row 5: *K3 with A, k3 with B; rep from *.

Row 7: *K3 with A, p3 with B; rep from *.

Rep Rows 1–8 for desired length.

2x2 Rib with Traveling Cable

(multiple of 18 sts + 6)

Row 1: (RS) *K2, p2, k2, *p3, 1/1RC, p2, 1/1RC, p3; rep from *, end k2, p2, k2.

Row 2, 4, 6, and 8: Knit the knits and purl the purls.

Row 3: *[K2, p2] 2 times, [1/1RCP, 1/1LCP] 2 times, p2; rep from *, end k2, p2, k2.

Row 5: *[K2, p2] 2 times, k1, p2, 1/1LC, p2, k1, p2; rep from *, end k2, p2, k2.

Row 7: *[K2, p2] 2 times, [1/1LCP, 1/1RCP] 2 times, p2; rep from *, end k2, p2, k2.

Rep Rows 1–8 for desired length.

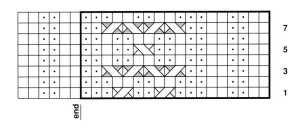

2x2 Two-Stitch Cable Rib

(multiple of 4 sts + 2)

Note : A Baby Cable (page 100) may be substituted for 1/1RC.

Row 1: (RS) *P2, k2; rep from *, end p2.

Rows 2 and 4: Knits the knits and purl the purls.

Row 3: *P2, 1/1RC; rep from *, end p2.

Rep Rows 1–4 for desired length.

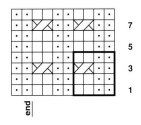

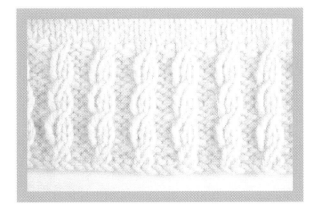

Two-Color Mock Cable Rib

(multiple of 5 sts + 2)

Mock cable: Knit 3rd st on left needle, knit 1st, then 2nd st, and drop all 3 sts from needle.

With A, CO desired number of sts.

Row 1: (RS) *P2 with A, work mock cable with B; rep from *, end p2 with A.

Rows 2 and 4: With established colors, knit the knits and purl the purls.

Row 3: *P2 with A, k3 with B; rep from *, end p2 with A.

Rep Rows 1–4 for desired length.

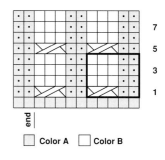

Color A   Color B

Baby Cable Rib

(multiple of 4 sts + 2)

Row 1: (RS) *P2, k2; rep from *, end p2.

Rows 2 and 4: K2, *p2, k2; rep from *.

Row 3: *P2, k2tog but leave sts on needle, knit the first st again, slip both sts off the needle; rep from *, end p2.

Rep Rows 1–4 for desired length.

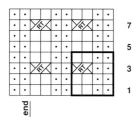

Graduated Baby Cable Rib

(multiple of 4 sts + 2)

Work Rows 1–4 of Baby Cable Rib (page 100) 2 times. Discontinue working 1 cable every 4 rows, or as desired, working these sts in 2 x 2 rib instead.

Pyramid Baby Cable Rib

(multiple of 4 sts + 2)

Work Rows 1–4 of Baby Cable Rib (page 100). Work 1 less cable each end of needle every 4 rows, or as desired, working these sts in rib instead so that cables form a pyramid shape.

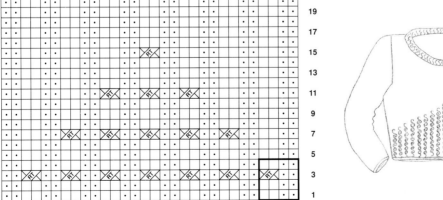

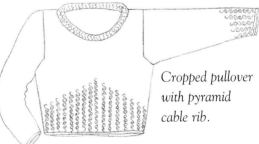

Cropped pullover with pyramid cable rib.

Three-Color Mock Cable Rib
(multiple of 15 sts + 2)

Mock cable: Knit 3rd st on left needle, knit 1st st, then
  2nd st, drop all 3 sts from needle.
With MC, CO desired number of sts.
Row 1: *P2 with MC, *work mock cable with A, p2 with
  MC, work mock cable with B, p2 with MC, work mock
  cable with C; rep from *, end p2 with MC.
Rows 2, 3, and 4: Knit the knits and purl the purls with
  established colors.
Rep Rows 1–4 for desired length.

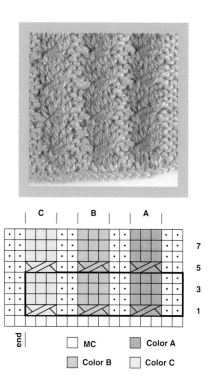

2x2 and Two-Stitch Cable Rib
(multiple of 8 sts + 6)

Row 1: (RS) *P2, k2; rep from *, end p2.
Rows 2 and 4: Knit the knits and purl the purls.
Row 3: *P2, k2, p2, *knit the 2nd st, then knit the
  1st st and slide both sts off the needle; rep from *,
  end p2, k2, p2.
Rep Rows 1–4 for desired length.

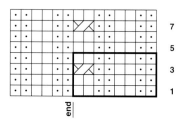

Four-Stitch Cable Rib

(multiple of 8 sts)

Row 1: *P2, k4, p2; rep from *.
Rows 2 and 4: Knit the knits and purl the purls.
Row 3: *P2, 2/2LC, p2; rep from *.
Rep Rows 1–4 for desired length.

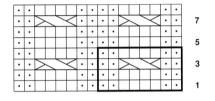

2x2 Rib with Double Four-Stitch Cables

(multiple of 20 sts + 6)

Row 1: (RS) *[K2, p2] 2 times, [k4, p2] 2
   times; rep from *, end k2, p2, k2.
Rows 2 and 4: Knit the knits and purl the
   purls.
Row 3: *[K2, p2] 2 times, 2/2LC, p2, 2/2LC,
   p2; rep from *, end k2, p2, k2.
Rep Rows 1–4 for desired length.

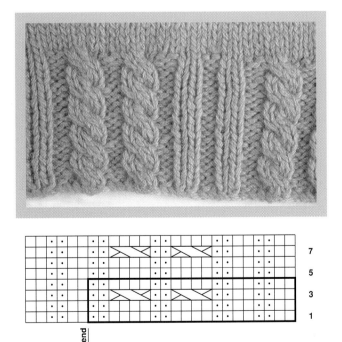

Cable and Bar Rib

(multiple of 10 sts + 8)

Rows 1 and 5: (RS) *P2, k4, p2, 1/1 LC; rep from *,
end p2, k4, p2.

Rows 2, 4, and 6: Knit the knits and purl the
purls.

Row 3: *P2, 2/2LC, p2, 1/1LC; rep from *, end p2,
2/2LC p2.

Rep Rows 1–6 for desired length.

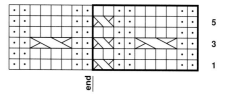

2x2 Mistake Rib

(multiple of 4 sts + 1)

Note: Sample shows 3-st seed st knit cord (page
150) sewn in place above rib.

Row 1: *P2, k2; rep from * end p1.

Row 2: *K2, p2; rep from *, end k1.

Rep Rows 1 and 2 for desired length.

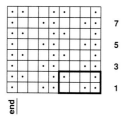

2x2 Shaded Rib

(multiple of 8 sts + 2)

Row 1: (RS) K3, *yo, ssk, k2; rep from *, end
last rep k3.

Row 2: P3, *yo, p2tog, p2; rep from *, end last
rep p3.

Rep Rows 1 and 2 once. Change colors and work
Rows 1–2 twice. Cont in this manner, changing
colors every 4 rows for desired length.

2x2 Vertical Bobble Rib

(multiple of 9 sts + 6)

Bobble (MB): ([k1f&b] 2 times, k1) in same st—5
sts, turn; [sl 1, k4, turn, sl 1, p4, turn] 2 times; pass
2nd, 3rd, 4th, and 5th st over 1st st on right needle—1 st.

Rows 1 and 5: (RS) K2, p2, k2, *p3, k2, p2, k2;
rep from *.

Rows 2, 4, and 6: Knit the knits and purl the
purls.

Row 3: K2, p2, k2, *p1, MB, p1, k2, p2, k2; rep
from *.

Rep Rows 1–6 for desired length.

Diagonal Bobble Rib

(multiple of 6 sts + 2)

Bobble (MB): ([K1f&b] 3 times) in same st—6 sts. Pass 2nd, 3rd, 4th, 5th, and 6th st over 1st st—1 st.

Row 1: K1, *k2, MB, p3; rep from *, end k1.

Row 2 and all even-numbered rows: K1, *k3, p3; rep from *, end last rep p4.

Row 3: K1, *p1, k2, MB, p2; rep from *, end k1.

Row 5: K1, *p2, k2, MB, p1; rep from *, end k1.

Row 7: K1, *p3, k2, MB; rep from *, end k1.

Row 9: K1, *MB, p3, k2; rep from *, end last rep k3.

Row 11: K1, *k1, MB, p3, k1; rep from *, end last rep k2.

Rep Rows 1–12 for desired length.

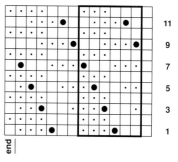

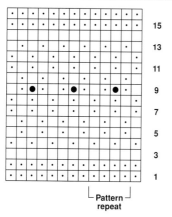

Double Seed Rib with Bobbles

(multiple of 4 sts + 1)

Bobble (MB): ([k1f&b] 2 times, k1) in same st—5 sts, turn; [sl 1, k4, turn, sl 1, p4, turn] 2 times; pass 2nd, 3rd, 4th, and 5th st over 1st st on right needle—1 st.

Rows 1 and 14: Purl.

Rows 2, 3, 15, and 16: Knit.

Rows 4, 5, 8, 12, and 13: K1, *p1, k1; rep from *.

Rows 6, 7, 10, and 11: P1, *k1, p1; rep from *.

Row 9: K1, *p1, MB, p1, k1; rep from *.

Vertical Bar and Bobble Rib with Bobble Edge

(multiple of 10 sts + 5)

Bobble (MB): ([K1, p1] 2 times, k1) in same st—5 sts, turn, p5, turn, k5, pass 2nd, 3rd, 4th, and 5th st over 1st st.

Row 1: (RS) P2, *MB, p4; rep from *, end MB, p2.

Rows 2, 4, and 6: Knit the knits and purl the purls.

Row 3: P2, *k1, p4; rep from *, end k1, p2.

Row 5: P2, *MB, p4, k1, p4; rep from *, end MB, p2.

Rep Rows 3–6 for desired length.

3x2 Center Bobble Rib

(multiple of 5 sts + 2)

Bobble (MB): ([K1, p1] 2 times, k1) in same st—5 sts, turn, p5, turn, k5, turn, p5, turn, pass 2nd, 3rd, 4th, and 5th st over 1st st—1 st.

Rows 1 and 3: P2, *k3, p2; rep from *.

Rows 2, 4, and 6: Knit the knits and purl the purls.

Row 5: P2, *k1, MB, k1, p2; rep from *.

Rep Rows 1–6 for desired length.

Mock Tassel Rib

(multiple of 7 sts + 2)

Row 1: (RS) P2, *k1b, [p1, k1b] 2 times, p2; rep from *.

Row 2: K2, *p1b, [k1, p1b] 2 times, k2; rep from *.

Rep Rows 1 and 2 for 2" (5 cm), end with Row 2.

Row 3: P2, *sl next 5 sts onto cn, wrap yarn counter-clockwise around cn snugly 4 times (page 264), sl these 5 sts back onto right needle, p2; rep from *.

Row 4: K2, *p5, k2; rep from *.

Row 5: P2, *k5, p2; rep from *.

Row 6: K2, *sl next st onto cn and hold in back, k1, p1 from cn, p1, sl next st onto cn and hold in front, p1, k1 from cn, k2; rep from *.

Row 7: P3, *M1, sl 2tog kwise, k1, p2sso, M1, p4; rep from *, end last rep p3.

Rows 8 and 10: K4, *p1, k6; rep from *, end last rep k4.

Row 9: P4, *k1, p6; rep from *, end last rep p4.

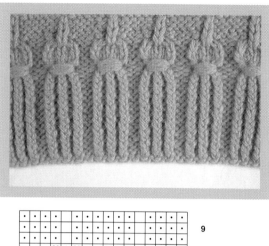

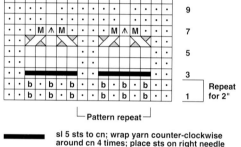

sl 5 sts to cn; wrap yarn counter-clockwise around cn 4 times; place sts on right needle

Six-Stitch Plait Rib

(multiple of 9 sts + 3)

Note: Sample shows rev St st knit cord (page 150) sewn above rib.

Row 1: (RS) P3, *2/2LC, k2, p3; rep from *.

Rows 2 and 4: Knit the knits and purl the purls.

Row 3: P3, *k2, 2/2RC, p3; rep from.

Rep Rows 1–4 for desired length.

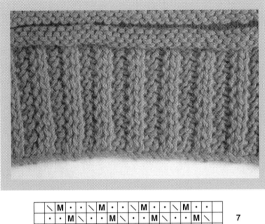

Density Rib with Roll

(multiple of 4 sts + 2)

Row 1: K1, *ssk, M1, p2; rep from *, end k1.
Row 2: P1, *ssp, M1, k2; rep from *, end p1.

Rep Rows 1 and 2 for desired length. Leave sts on needle and insert a fine circular needle through all sts. To make roll, cont with original needle and work St st for 1" (2.5 cm). BO all sts. Join yarn and with original needle, knit sts held on circular needle. Cont in desired patt for desired length.

5x3 Rib with Daisy Stitch

(multiple of 8 sts + 3)

Row 1: (RS) P3, *k5, p3; rep from *.
Row 2: K3, *p5, k3; rep from *.
Rep Rows 1 and 2 for desired length.
Embroider daisy st (page 202) over each group of
   5 knit sts.

5x2 Rib with Button Embellishment

(multiple of 7 sts + 2)

Row 1: (RS) P2, *k5, p2; rep from *.
Row 2: K2, *p5, k2; rep from *.
Rep Rows 1 and 2 for desired length.
Sew button onto every other group of 5 knit sts.

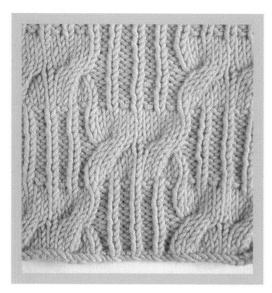

1x2 Rib and Cable Block

(multiple of 24 sts + 13 + 2 edge sts)

Rows 1, 3, 5, 9, and 11: K1, *k13, [p2, k1] 3 times, p2; rep from *, end k14.

Row 2 and all even-numbered rows: Knit the knits and purl the purls.

Row 7: K1, *3/3RC, k1, 3/3RC, [p2, k1] 3 times, p2; rep from *, end [3/3RC, k1] 2 times.

Rows 13, 15, 17, 21, and 23: K2, *[p2, k1] 3 times, p2, k13; rep from *, end [p2, k1] 4 times, k1.

Row 19: K2, *[p2, k1] 3 times, p2, 3/3RC, k1, 3/3RC; rep from *, end [p2, k1] 4 times, k1.

Rep Rows 1–24 for desired length.

Many ribs can be used as allover patterns. In this design a 1 × 2 rib and cable block is combined with a graduated rib.

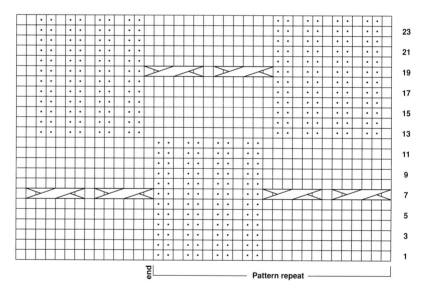

1x2 Rib to V-Point

(multiple of 28 sts + 1)

Beg with p2, work k1, p2 rib for desired length.

Row 1: (RS) *P1, k3, p1, [k1, p2] 6 times, k1, p1, k3, p1; rep from *, end p1.

Row 2 and all even-numbered rows through 26: Knit the knits and purl the purls.

Row 3: *P1, 3/1LCP, [k1, p2] 6 times, k1, 3/1RCP; rep from *, end p1.

Row 5: *P2, 3/1LCP, [p2, k1] 5 times, p2, 3/1RCP, p1; rep from *; end last rep p2.

Row 7: *P3, 3/1LCP, p1, [k1, p2] 4 times, k1, p1, 3/1RCP, p2; rep from *, end last rep p3.

Row 9: *P4, 3/1LCP, [k1, p2] 4 times, k1, 3/1RCP, p3; rep from *, end last rep p4.

Row 11: *P5, 3/1LCP, [p2, k1] 3 times, p2, 3/1RCP, p4; rep from *, end last rep p5.

Row 13: *P6, 3/1LCP, p1, [k1, p2] 2 times, k1, p1, 3/1RCP, p5; rep from *, end last rep p6.

Row 15: *P7, 3/1LCP, [k1, p2] 2 times, k1, 3/1RCP, p6; rep from *, end last rep p7.

Row 17: *P8, 3/1LCP, p2, k1, p2, 3/1RCP, p7; rep from *, end last rep p8.

Row 19: *P9, 3/1LCP, p1, k1, p1, 3/1RCP, p8; rep from *, end last rep p9.

Row 21: *P10, 3/1LCP, k1, 3/1RCP, p9; rep from *, end last rep p10.

Row 23: *P11, M1, k2, sl 2 (1 at a time) kwise, k1, p2sso, k2, M1, p10; rep from *, end last rep p11.

Row 25: *P12, M1, k1, sl 2 (1 at a time) kwise, k1, p2sso, k1, M1, p11; rep from *, end last rep p12.

Row 27: *P13, M1, sl 2 (1 at a time) kwise, k1, p2sso, M1, p12; rep from *, end last rep p13.

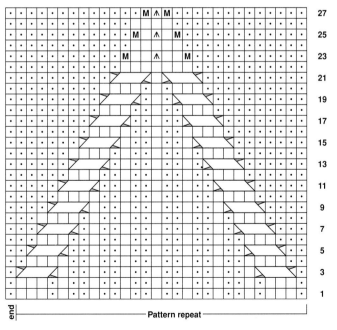

Bell Cable Rib

(multiple of 14 sts + 2)

Rows 1, 3, 5, 7, and 9: (RS) *P2, k2, [p3, k2] 2 times; rep from *, end p2.

Row 2 and all even-numbered rows: Knit the knits and purl the purls.

Row 11: *P2, 2/3LCP, k2, 2/3RCP; rep from *, end p2.

Rows 13, 15, 17, and 21: Knit the knits and purl the purls.

Row 19: P1, *P4, *3/3LC, p8, 3/3RC, p4; rep from *, end last rep p5.

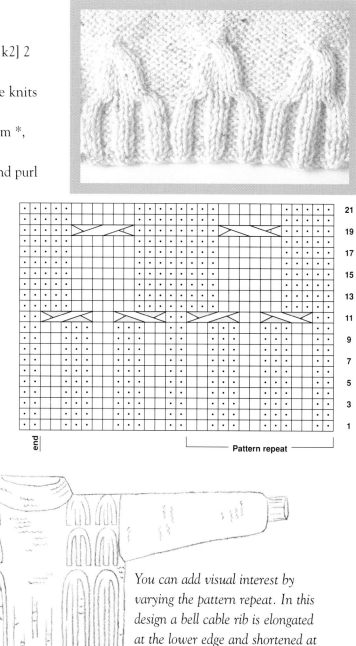

You can add visual interest by varying the pattern repeat. In this design a bell cable rib is elongated at the lower edge and shortened at the shoulder.

Uneven Edgings

Picots, points, scallops, and bobbles on the edges of garments can make dramatic statements. Uneven edges are formed with increase and decrease combinations. Some are knitted horizontally, some vertically, some are knitted in pieces and then joined together, some are layered, and some are created with a simple twist. These basic uneven edges can be used for beautiful corners, frames, and flowers.

Picot Hem

(multiple of 2 sts + 1)

This edging may be used on CO or BO edge.

Rows 1–4: Work in St st.

Row 5: (RS; picot row) K1, *yo, k2tog; rep from *.

Rows 6–9: Beg with a WS row, work in St st. Fold along picot row and sew in place.

```
                                    9

                                    7

        / O / O / O                 5

                                    3

                                    1
```

Picot Point Chain Edgings

Work this edging on the last row of a knitted piece. The sample is embellished with pearl beads and embroidered daisy st (page 202).

BO 2 sts, *sl rem st on right needle to left needle, using the cable method (page 259), CO 3 sts, then BO 5 sts; rep from * until 1 st rem. Fasten off.

Picot Chain Loops

(multiple of 5 sts)

(Worked separately and attached to knitted edge.)

Row 1: Knit.

Row 2: BO 2 sts, *sl rem st on right needle to left needle, [using the cable method (page 259), CO 2 sts, BO next 2 sts, sl rem st on right needle to left needle] 3 times, cable CO 2 sts, BO 6 sts; rep from *.

Picot Lace with Ribbon

(multiple of 3 sts + 2)

Row 1: (RS) Sl 1, k1 *yo, p2tog, (k1, p1, k1) in next st; rep from *—4 sts inc'd.

Row 2: *K3, yo, p2tog; rep from *, end k2.

Row 3: Sl 1, k1, *yo, p2tog, k3; rep from *.

Row 4: *BO 2 sts kwise, yo, p2tog; rep from *, end k2.

Rep Rows 1–4 for desired length. Weave ribbon through picots.

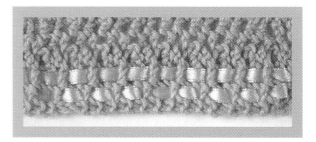

Cast-on

■ no stitch

Casey's Picot Point

(multiple of 20 sts + 1)

CO using the provisional method (page 259).

Rows 1, 2, and 3: Beg with a knit row, work St st.

Row 4: (WS) P1, *yo, p2tog; rep from *.

Rows 5, 6, and 7: Beg with a knit row, work St st.

Row 8: (WS) Place CO sts on a spare dpn and place in front of and parallel to working needle. Fold at picot edge. P2tog (1 st from each needle) across row.

Row 9: *K1, yo, [p1, k1b] 4 times, sl 1 pwise, k2tog, psso, [k1b, p1] 4 times, yo; rep from *, end k1.

Row 10: P1, *p1, yo, [k1, p1b] 3 times, k1, sl 1 kwise, p2tog, psso, k1, [p1b, k1] 3 times, yo, p2; rep from *.

Row 11: *K3, yo, [p1, k1b] 3 times, sl 1 pwise, k2tog, psso, [k1b, p1] 3 times, yo, k2; rep from *, end last rep k3.

Row 12: P1, *p3, yo, [k1, p1b] 2 times, k1, sl 1 kwise, p2tog, psso, k1, [p1b, k1] 2 times, yo, p4; rep from *.

Row 13: *K5, yo, [p1, k1b] 2 times, sl 1 pwise, k2tog, psso, [k1b, p1] 2 times, yo, k4; rep from *, end last rep k5.

Row 14: P1, *p5, yo, k1, p1b, k1, sl 1 kwise, p2tog, psso, k1, p1b, k1, yo, p6; rep from *.

Row 15: *K7, yo, p1, k1b, sl 1 pwise, k2tog, psso, k1b, p1, yo, k6; rep from *, end last rep k7.

Row 16: P1, *p7, yo, k1, sl 1 kwise, p2tog, psso, k1, yo, p8; rep from *.

Row 17: *K9, yo, sl 1 pwise, k2tog, psso, yo, k8; rep from *, end last rep k9.

Row 18: Purl.

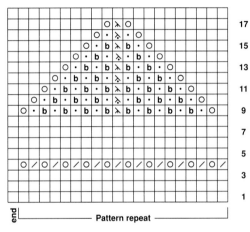

Use provisional cast-on
Note : On Row 8, work sts tog with live CO sts.

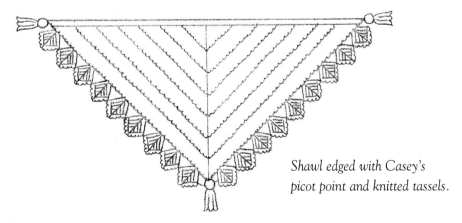

Shawl edged with Casey's picot point and knitted tassels.

Victoria's Lace Picot

(multiple of 15 sts + 6)

CO using the provisional method (page 259).

Rows 1–3 and 5–7: Beg with a knit row, work St st.

Row 4: P1, *yo, p2tog; rep from *.

Row 8: (WS) Place CO sts on a spare dpn and place in front of and parallel to working needle. Fold at picot edge. P2tog (1 st from each needle) across row.

Row 9: (RS) K1, *k2, yo, ssk, yo, [k1b, p1] 2 times, sl 1 kwise, k2tog, psso, [p1, k1b] 2 times, yo; rep from *, end k2tog, yo, k3.

Row 10: P1, p2tog, yo, p2, *p1b, yo, p1b, k1, p1b, sl 1 kwise, p2tog, psso, p1b, k1, p1b, yo, p1b; rep form *, end p2, yo, p1.

Row 11: K1, *k2, yo, ssk, k1b, p1, yo, k1b, p1, sl 1 kwise, k2tog, psso, p1, k1b, yo, p1, k1b; rep from *, end k2tog, yo, k3.

Row 12: P1, *p2tog, yo, p2, *p1b, k1, p1b, yo, p1b, sl 1 kwise, p2tog, psso, p1b, yo, p1b, k1, p1b, p2, yo, ssp; rep from *, end p1.

Row 13: K1, *k2, yo, ssk, [k1b, p1] 2 times, yo, sl 1 kwise, k2tog, psso, yo, [p1, k1b] 2 times; rep from *, end k2tog, yo, k3.

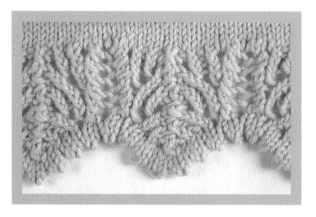

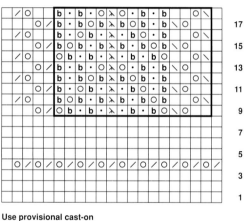

Use provisional cast-on
Note : On Row 8, work sts tog with live CO sts.

Row 14: P1, p2tog, yo, p2, *yo, [p1b, k1] 2 times, sl 1 kwise, p2tog, psso, [k1, p1b] 2 times, yo, p2, yo, ssp; rep from *, end p1.

Row 15: K1, *k2, yo, ssk, k1b, yo, k1b, p1, k1b, sl 1 kwise, k2tog, psso, k1b, p1, k1b, yo, k1b; rep from *, end k2tog, yo, k3.

Row 16: P1, p2tog, yo, p2, *p1b, k1, yo, p1b, k1, sl 1 kwise, p2tog, psso, k1, p1b, yo, k1, p1b, p2, yo, ssp; rep *, end p1.

Row 17: K1, *k2, yo, ssk, k1b, p1, k1b, yo, k1b, sl 1 kwise, k2tog, psso, k1b, yo, k1b, p1, k1b; rep from *, end k2tog, yo, k3.

Row 18: P1, p2tog, yo, p2, *[p1b, k1] 2 times, yo, sl 1 kwise, p2tog, psso, yo, [k1, p1b] 2 times, p2, yo, ssp; rep from *, end p1.

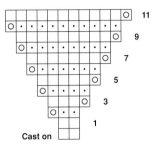

Basic Horizontal Points

Note: Each point is worked separately, then all points are joined on the same row.

CO 2 sts.

Row 1: K2.

Rows 2–11: YO, knit to end—11 sts after Row 11.

Rows 1–11 form 1 point. Break yarn and leave sts on needle. On the same needle, CO 2 sts and work another point. Cont in this manner until there are desired number of points on needle. Do not break yarn after last point, but turn and knit across all points on needle to join.

Solid Points with Knit Cord and Bobbles

Bobble: CO 1 st. ([K1f&b] 2 times) in same st—4 sts. Turn, work 4 rows St st. With left needle, lift 2nd, 3rd, and 4th sts over 1st st—1 st.

Work Basic Horizontal Points (above) until each point is 10 sts wide. Break yarn on all but last point. Cont even across all sts in garter st for desired length. With CC, work knit cord (page 149) and bobbles. Sew cord onto point from back of work. Attach bobbles to center of each point.

Stripe Points

Alternating colors as desired, work Basic Horizontal Points (above) until each point is 10 sts wide. Do not break yarn. Cont even in garter st on these sts, working colors as established and twisting color changes at back of work to prevent holes.

Multi-Point Overlay

With background color, work garter st for 1½" (3.8 cm). BO all sts. Work Basic Horizontal Points (page 117) in alternating colors until each point is 10 sts wide. On last row, break yarn after each color. BO in background color and sew points to garter-st background strip along BO edge.

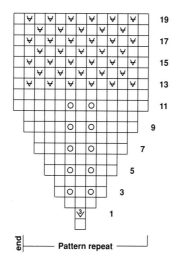

Dew Drops

Bobble cluster:

CO 1 st.

Row 1 (RS): ([K1, p1] 2 times, k1) in same st—5 sts.

Row 2, 4, 6, and 8: Sl 1, p4.

Row 3, 5, and 7: Sl 1, k4.

Row 9: K2tog, k1, k2tog—3 sts.

Row 10: P3tog, turn. Fold bobble in half. Insert left needle into CO st and knit it tog with the rem st of bobble—1 st.

Work Rows 1–10 two more times, leaving last st on needle.

Point:

Row 1: (RS) (K1f&b, k1) in rem st of bobble—3 sts.

Row 2, 4, 6, 8, 10, and 12: Purl.

Row 3: K1, [yo, k1] 2 times—5 sts.

Row 5: K2, yo, k1, yo, k2—7 sts.

Row 7: K3, yo, k1, yo, k3—9 sts.

Row 9: K4, yo, k1, yo, k4—11 sts.

Row 11: K5, yo, k1, yo, k5—13 sts.

Break yarn on all but last point and leave sts on needle.

end | Pattern repeat

Rep Rows 1–12 for each point. When all points are complete, turn. Knit 1 row, purl 1 row.

Then work pattern band as follows, slipping all sts pwise:

Rows 13, 15, 17, and 19: K1, *yf, sl 1, yb, k1; rep from *.

Rows 14, 16, and 18: P2, *yb, sl 1, yf, p1; rep from *, end last rep p2.

Sugar Drops

Work bobble clusters (page 118). Then work point as follows:

Row 1: (RS) (K1, yo, k1) in rem st of bobble— 3 sts.

Rows 2, 4, 6, 8, and 10: Purl.

Row 3: K1, [yo, k1] 2 times—5 sts.

Row 5: K1, yo, k3, yo, k1—7 sts.

Row 7: K1, yo, k5, yo, k1—9 sts.

Row 9: K1, yo, k7, yo, k1—11 sts.

Row 11: K1, yo, k9, yo, k1—13 sts.

Break yarn on all but last point and leave sts on needle. Rep from Row 1 for each point. Work rem rows across all sts.

Work pattern band as follows:

Rows 12 and 14: Purl.

Row 13: Knit.

Rows 15, 16, 19, and 20: *K1, p1; rep from *, end k1.

Rows 17, 18, and 21: *P1, k1; rep from *, end p1.

Sew beads in center of each point and above pattern band.

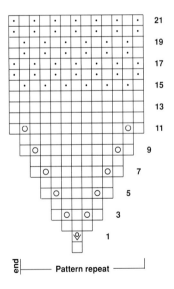

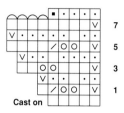

Cast on

Eyelet Points

CO 5 sts.

Row 1: (WS) Sl 1, k1, [yo] 2 times, k2tog, k1—
6 sts.

Row 2: Sl 1, k2, p1, k2.

Row 3: Sl 1, k3, [yo] 2 times, k2—8 sts.

Row 4: Sl 1, k2, p1, k4.

Row 5: Sl 1, k1, [yo] 2 times, k2tog, k4—9 sts.

Row 6: Sl 1, k5, p1, k2.

Row 7: Sl 1, k8.

Row 8: BO 4, k4—5 sts.

Rep Rows 1–8 for desired length, working the
points in different colors, if desired.

Saw-Tooth Points

CO 6 sts.

Row 1: (RS) K3, yo, k3—7 sts.

Rows 2, 4, 6, 8, and 10: Knit.

Row 3: K3, yo, k4—8 sts.

Row 5: K3, yo, k5—9 sts.

Row 7: K3, yo, k6—10 sts.

Row 9: K3, yo, k7—11 sts.

Row 11: K3, yo, k8—12 sts.

Row 12: BO 6 sts, k5—6 sts.

Rep Rows 1–12 for desired length.

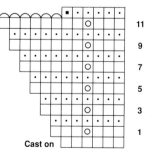

Cast on

Saw-Tooth Points with Bobbles

Make Bobble (MB): ([K1, p1] 2 times, k1) in next st,
  [turn, sl 1, k4] 4 times, pass first 4 sts over the last st.
CO 6 sts. Work Rows 1–10 of Saw-Tooth Points (page
  120).
Row 11: K3, yo, k7, MB—12 sts.
Row 12: BO 6 sts, k5—6 sts.
Rep Rows 1–12 for desired length.

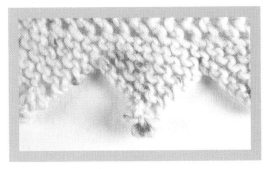

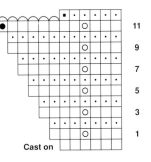

Vertical Eyelets with Ribbon

(multiple of 10 sts + 2)

Row 1: (RS) *K2, yo, k2tog, k4, ssk, yo; rep from *,
  end k2.
Row 2: Purl.
Rep Rows 1 and 2 for desired length. Thread
ribbon through eyelets, if desired.

Broken Eyelet

(multiple of 14 sts + 1)

Rows 1, 2, and 3: Knit.

Rows 4, 6, 8, 10, 12, and 14: Purl.

Rows 5, 7, 9, 11, and 13: (RS) *K1, yo, k3, ssk, yo, sl 1 kwise, k2tog, psso, yo, k2tog, k3, yo; rep from *, end k1.

Rows 15 and 16: Purl.

Rep Rows 5–16 for desired length.

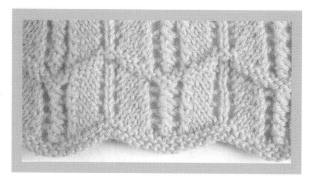

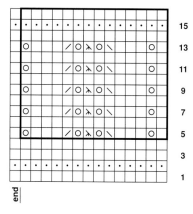

Feather Lace

(multiple of 9 sts + 4)

Rows 1, 2, and 3: Knit.

Rows 4, 6, and 8: Purl.

Row 5: (RS) K3, *yo, k2, ssk, k2tog, k2, yo, k1; rep from *, end last rep k2.

Row 7: K2, *yo, k2, ssk, k2tog, k2, yo, k1; rep from *, end last rep k3.

Rep Rows 5–8 for desired length.

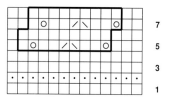

Angel's Edging

(multiple of 11 sts)

Rows 1, 3, and 5: (RS) Purl.

Rows 2, 4, and 6: Knit.

Row 7: *K2tog, k3, yo, k1, yo, k3, k2tog; rep from *.

Row 8: Purl.

Rep Rows 7 and 8 for desired length, end on Row 8. Purl 1 row, knit 1 row.

Heaven's Gate

(multiple of 18 sts + 1)

Row 1: (RS) *K1, yo, k5, k2tog, yo, sl 1 kwise, k2tog, psso, yo, ssk, k5, yo; rep from *, end k1.

Rows 2, 4, 6, and 8: Purl.

Row 3: *[K1, yo] 2 times, ssk, k2, k2tog, yo, sl 1 kwise, k2tog, psso, yo, ssk, k2, k2tog, yo, k1, yo; rep from *, end k1.

Row 5: *K1, yo, k3, yo, ssk, k2tog, yo, sl 1 kwise, k2tog, psso, yo, ssk, k2tog, yo, k3, yo; rep from *, end k1.

Row 7: *K1, yo, k5, yo, ssk, sl 1 kwise, k2tog, psso, k2tog, yo, k5, yo; rep from *, end k1.

Rep Rows 1–8 for desired length.

Note: Sample has 3-st knit cord (page 149) sewn to CO edge.

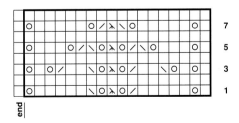

Fan Dance

(cast on multiple of 19 sts)

Rows 1 and 2: Knit.

Row 3: *K1, [yo] 2 times, ssp, k13, p2tog, [yo] 2 times, k1; rep from *—mult of 21 sts.

Row 4: *K1, (k1, p1) in "[yo] 2 times," k15, (p1, k1) in "[yo] 2 times," k1; rep from *.

Rows 5 and 6: Knit.

Row 7: *K1, [(yo) 2 times, ssp] 2 times, k11, [p2tog, (yo) 2 times] 2 times, k1; rep from *— mult of 25 sts.

Row 8: *[K1, (k1, p1) in "[yo] 2 times"] 2 times, k13, [(p1, k1) in "[yo] 2 times," k1] 2 times; rep from *.

Row 9: Knit.

Row 10: *K6, [(yo) 2 times, k1] 14 times, k5; rep from *—mult of 53 sts.

Row 11: *K1, [(yo) 2 times, ssp] 2 times, [yo] 2 times, dropping extra yo's of previous row, p15tog, [yo] 2 times, [p2tog, (yo) 2 times] 2 times, k1; rep from *—mult of 19 sts.

Row 12: *K1, [p1, k1] 4 times, k1, [k1, p1] 4 times, k1; rep from *.

Sew beads to CO edge.

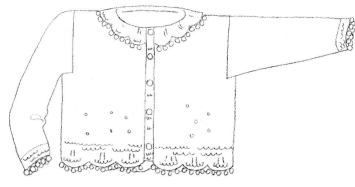

Use the fan dance edging for a dressy look.

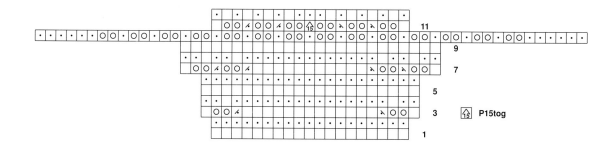

Arbor Lace with Tassels and Embroidery

(cast on multiple of 11 sts)

Row 1: (RS) *Ssk, [k1b] 3 times, yo, k1, yo, [k1b] 3 times, k2tog; rep from *.

Rows 2, 4, 6, and 8: Purl.

Row 3: *Ssk, [k1b] 2 times, yo, k1, yo, ssk, yo, [k1b] 2 times, k2tog; rep from *.

Row 5: *Ssk, k1b, yo, k1, [yo, ssk] 2 times, yo, k1b, k2tog; rep from *.

Row 7: *Ssk, yo, k1, [yo, ssk] 3 times, yo, k2tog; rep from *.

Row 9: *K1, p1, k7, p1, k1; rep from *.

Row 10: Knit the knits and purl the purls.

Rep Rows 9 and 10 for desired length. BO all sts. Make 4" (10-cm) tassel (page 221) for each point. Embroider diagonal straight st (page 192) over center 2 knit sts above each tassel.

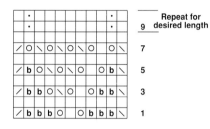

Gazebo Lace

(cast on multiple of 10 sts + 1)

Bobble (MB): (p1, k1, p1) in next st, [turn, k1, p1, k1] 2 times, pass 2nd and 3rd st over 1st st.

Set-up row: (WS) P5, *MB, p4; rep from *, end last rep p5.

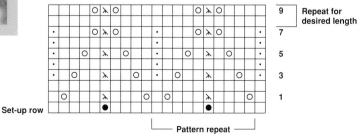

Row 1: (RS) K1, *yo, k3, sl 1 kwise, k2tog, psso, k3, yo, k1; rep from *.

Row 2: Purl.

Row 3: P1, *k1, yo, k2, sl 1 kwise, k2tog, psso, k2, yo, k1, p1; rep from *.

Rows 4 and 6: *K1, p9; rep from *, end k1.

Row 5: P1, *k2, yo, k1, sl 1 kwise, k2tog, psso, k1, yo, k2, p1; rep from *.

Row 7: P1, *k3, yo, sl 1 kwise, k2tog, psso, yo, k3, p1; rep from *.

Row 8: Purl.

Row 9: K1, *k3, yo, sl 1 kwise, k2tog, psso, yo, k4; rep from *.

Rep Rows 1–9, then rep Rows 8 and 9 for desired length.

Festive Mimosa

(cast on multiple of 24 sts + 4)

Bobble (MB): ([K1f&b] 2 times) in same st—4 sts, turn, p4, turn, k4, pass 2nd, 3rd, and 4th st over 1st st.

Rows 1 and 3: (RS) With CC, purl.

Row 2: with CC, knit.

Row 4: Change to MC, purl.

Row 5: K1, k2tog, *[k1, yo] 2 times, k7, sl 2tog kwise, k1, p2sso, k7, [yo, k1] 2 times, sl 2tog kwise, k1, p2sso; rep from * to last 3 sts, ssk, k1.

Rows 6, 8, 10, 12, 14, and 16: Purl.

Row 7: K1, k2tog, *k2, [yo, k1] 2 times, k1, MB, k3, sl 2tog kwise, k1, p2sso, k3, MB, k2, [yo, k1] 2 times, k1, sl 2tog kwise, k1, p2sso; rep from * to last 3 sts, ssk, k1.

Row 9: K1, k2tog, *MB, k2, [yo, k1] 2 times, k1, MB, k2, sl 2tog kwise, k1, p2sso, k2, MB, k2, [yo, k1] 2 times, k1, MB, sl 2tog kwise, k1, p2sso; rep from * to last 3 sts, ssk, k1.

Row 11: K1, k2tog, *k1, MB, k2, [yo, k1] 2 times, k1, MB, k1, sl 2tog kwise, k1, p2sso, k1, MB, k2, [yo, k1] 2 times, k1, MB, k1, sl 2tog kwise, k1, p2sso; rep from * to last 3 sts, ssk, k1.

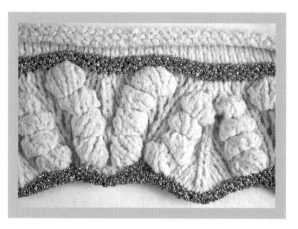

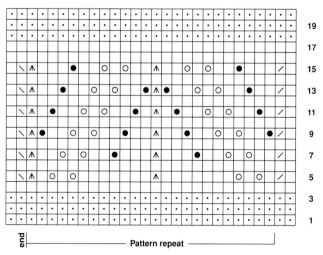

Row 13: K1, k2tog, *k2, MB, k2, [yo, k1] 2 times, k1, MB, sl 2tog kwise, k1, p2sso, MB, k2, [yo, k1] 2 times, k1, MB, k2, sl 2tog kwise, k1, p2sso; rep from * to last 3 sts, ssk, k1.

Row 15: K1, k2tog, *k3, MB, k2, [yo, k1] 2 times, k1, sl 2tog kwise, k1, p2sso, k2, [yo, k1] 2 times, k1, MB, k3, sl 2tog kwise, k1, p2sso; rep from * to last 3 sts, ssk, k1.

Rows 17, 18, and 20: With CC, knit.

Row 19: With CC, Purl.

Brunhilda's Broom Border

(cast on multiple of 21 sts + 3)

Set-up: Work 3 rows rev St st.

Row 1: (RS) K1, *yo, k21; rep from *, end last rep k23—mult of 22 sts + 3.

Row 2: P2, *[p1, k3] 5 times, p2; rep from *, end last rep p3.

Row 3: K1, *k1, yo, k1, [p3, k1] 5 times, yo; rep from *, end k2—mult of 24 sts + 3.

Row 4: P2, *p3, [k3, p1] 5 times, p1; rep from *, end last rep p3.

Row 5: K1, *[k1, yo] 2 times, [ssk, p2] 5 times, [k1, yo] 2 times; rep from *, end k2—mult of 23 sts + 3.

Row 6: P2, *p4, [k2, p1] 5 times, p4; rep from *, end last rep p5.

Row 7: K1, *[k1, yo] 4 times, [ssk, p1] 5 times, [k1, yo] 4 times; rep from *, end k2—mult of 26 sts + 3.

Row 8: P2, *p8, [k1, p1] 5 times, p8; rep from *, end last rep p9.

Row 9: K1, *k8, [ssk] 5 times, k8; rep from *, end last rep k10—mult of 21 sts + 3.

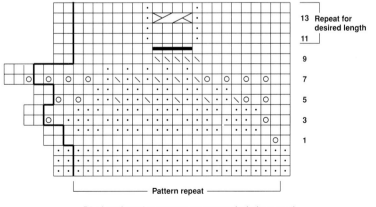

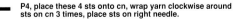

P4, place these 4 sts onto cn, wrap yarn clockwise around sts on cn 3 times, place sts on right needle.

Row 10: P2, **p8, p4, place these 4 sts on cn, wrap yarn clockwise around sts on cn 3 times (page 264), place sts from cn onto right needle, p9; rep from *, end last rep p10.*

Row 11: K1, **k8, p1, k4, p1, k7; rep from *, end last rep k9.*

Rows 12 and 14: Knit the knits and purl the purls.

Row 13: K1, **k8, p1, 2/2RC, p1, k7; rep from *, end last rep k9.*

Rep Rows 11–14 for desired length.

Double Bear Paws and Cord

(cast on multiple of 16 sts + 1)

Note: Sample shows knit cord (page 149) sewn above rib.

Row 1: (RS) K1, **yo, [k1, p1] 7 times, k1, yo, k1; rep from *—mult of 18 sts + 1.*

Row 2: K1, **p2, [k1, p1] 7 times, p1, k1; rep from *.*

Row 3: K2, **yo, [k1, p1] 7 times, k1, yo, k3; rep from *, end last rep k2—mult of 20 sts + 1.*

Row 4: K2, **p2, [k1, p1] 7 times, p1, k3; rep from *, end last rep k2.*

Row 5: K3, **yo, [k1, p1] 7 times, k1, yo, k5; rep from *, end last rep k3—mult of 22 sts + 1.*

Row 6: K3, **p2, [k1, p1] 7 times, p1, k5; rep from *, end last rep k3.*

Row 7: K4, **yo, [k1, p1] 7 times, k1, yo, k7; rep from *, end last rep k4—mult of 24 sts + 1.*

Row 8: K4, **p2, [k1, p1] 7 times, p1, k7; rep from *, end last rep k4.*

Row 9: K5, **[ssk] 3 times, sl 1 kwise, k2tog, psso, [k2tog] 3 times, k9; rep from *, end last rep k5—mult of 16 sts + 1.*

Row 10: Purl.

Several rows of the double bear paws edging are combined with an eyelet pattern, scalloped edging, and knit cord in this design.

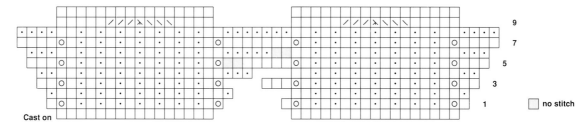

Bear Tracks

(multiple of 23 sts)

Row 1: (RS) *K2, (p4, k1) 3 times, p4, k2; rep from *.

Row 2 and all even-numbered rows: Knit the knits and purl the purls.

Row 3: *K1, yo, k1, p2, p2tog, (k1, p4) 2 times, k1, p2tog, p2, k1, yo, k1; rep from *.

Row 5: *K2, yo, k1, p3, k1, p2, p2tog, k1, p2tog, p2, k1, p3, k1, yo, k2; rep from *.

Row 7: *K3, yo, k1, p1, p2tog, [k1, p3] 2 times, k1, p2tog, p1, k1, yo, k3; rep from *.

Row 9: *K4, yo, k1, p2, k1, p1, p2tog, k1, p2tog, p1, k1, p2, k1, yo, k4; rep from *.

Row 11: *K5, yo, k1, p2tog, [k1, p2] 2 times, k1, p2tog, k1, yo, k5; rep from *.

Row 13: *K6, yo, k1, p1, k1, [p2tog, k1] 2 times, p1, k1, yo, k6; rep from *.

Row 14: Knit the knits and purl the purls.

Note: Sample shows 3 rows rev St st after Row 14.

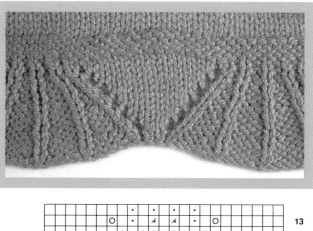

Petite Shells

(cast on multiple of 5 sts + 2)

Row 1: (RS) K1, yo, *k5, sl the 2nd, 3rd, 4th, and 5th st over the 1st st, yo; rep from * to last st, k1—mult of 2 sts + 3.

Row 2: P1, *(p1, yo, k1b) in same st, p1; rep from *—mult of 4 sts + 1.

Row 3: K2, k1b, *k3, k1b; rep from * to last 2 sts, k2.

Rows 4–6: Knit.

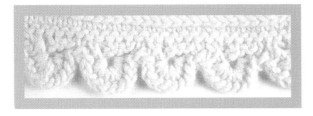

Sugar Scallops

(cast on multiple of 11 sts + 2)

Row 1: (RS) Purl.

Row 2: K2, *k1 and sl back onto left needle, lift the next 8 sts, 1 at a time, over this st and off needle, [yo] 2 times, knit the 1st st again, k2; rep from *—mult of 5 sts + 2.

Row 3: K1, *p2tog, drop one loop of "[yo] 2 times" of previous row, ([k1f&b] 2 times, k1) in rem loop, p1; rep from * to last st, k1—mult of 7 sts + 2.

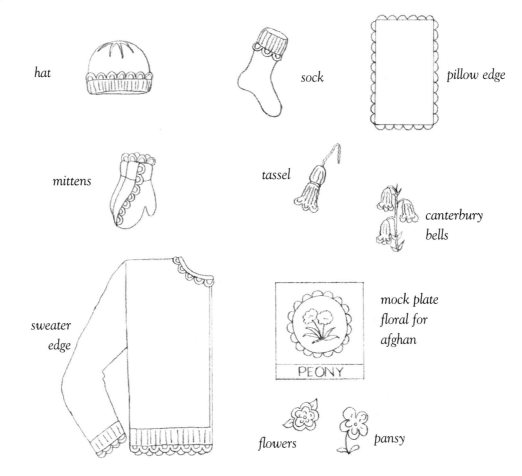

hat

sock

pillow edge

mittens

tassel

canterbury bells

sweater edge

mock plate floral for afghan

PEONY

flowers

pansy

There are several ways to interpret a single edging. Shown here are ten ideas for using sugar scallops.

Lacy Shells

(cast on multiple of 5 sts + 2)

Row 1: (RS) K1, yo, *k5, slip the 2nd, 3rd, 4th, and 5th st over the 1st st, yo; rep from * to last st, k1—mult of 2 sts + 3.

Row 2: P1, *(p1, yo, k1b) in same st, p1; rep from *— mult of 4 sts + 1.

Row 3: K2, k1b, *k3, k1b; rep from * to last 2 sts, k2.

Row 4: Knit.

Rows 5, 6, and 7: K1, *yo, k2tog; rep from *.

Row 8: Knit.

Thread ribbon through holes.

Scalloped Edging with Rib

(multiple of 11 sts + 2)

Row 1: (WS) Purl.

Row 2: K2, *k1, sl this st back to left needle, lift the next 8 sts on left needle over this st and off needle, [yo] 2 times, knit the first st again, k2; rep from *.

Row 3: K1, *p2tog, drop extra loop, [k1f&b] 2 times in rem yo of previous row, p1; rep from * to last st, k1—mult of 6 sts + 2.

Row 4: *K1, p1; rep from *.

Row 5: *P1, k1; rep from *.

Rep Rows 4 and 5 for desired length.

Horizontal Garter-Stitch Scallops

CO 5 sts for each scallop.

Row 1: K5, CO 1 st.

   Cont to inc 1 st each row until each scallop is 12 sts, or desired width. Break yarn on all but the last scallop. Work 4 rows garter st over all scallops. BO all sts, or cont in patt st.

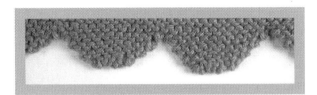

Vertical Garter-Stitch Scallops

Note: The CO edge is at the right side of the photo.

CO 7 sts. Knit 1 row.

Row 1: K5, k1f&b, k1—8 sts.

Row 2: K1, k1f&b, k6—9 sts.

Row 3: K7, k1f&b, k1—10 sts.

Row 4: K1, k1f&b, k8—11 sts.

Row 5: K9, k1f&b, k1—12 sts.

Row 6: K1, k1f&b, k10—13 sts.

Row 7: K11, k1f&b, k1—14 sts.

Row 8: K1, k1f&b, k12—15 sts.

Row 9: K12, k2tog, k1—14 sts.

Row 10: K1, k2tog, k11—13 sts.

Row 11: K10, k2tog, k1—12 sts.

Row 12: K1, k2tog, k9—11 sts.

Row 13: K8, k2tog, k1—10 sts.

Row 14: K1, k2tog, k7—9 sts.

Row 15: K6, k2tog, k1—8 sts.

Row 16: K1, k2tog, k5—7 sts.

Rep Rows 1–16 for desired length.

Other Edgings

Vertical

These vertically knitted borders use small stitch counts and row repeats. Because the number of stitches cast on determines the width of the borders, you can simply repeat the pattern until the piece is the length you want

Boxcars

Note: The CO edge is at the right side of the photo.

CO 15 sts.

Hint: Mark the first sl st on the Set-up row and Rows 2, 4, 6, 8, and 10.

Set-up row: (WS) Sl 1, k2, p9, k3.

Row 1: Sl 1, k1, p1, k5, k2tog, yo, k2, p1, k2.

Rows 2, 4, 6, 8, 10, and 12: Sl 1, k2, p9, k3.

Row 3: Sl 1, k1, p1, k4, k2tog, yo, k3, p1, k2.

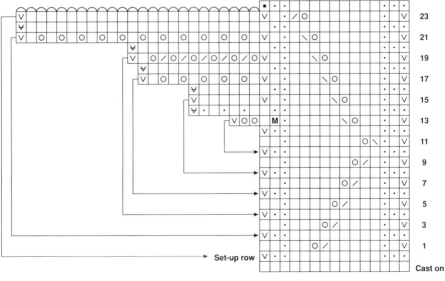

→ Pick up st at end of indicated row, knit it, and pass slipped st from current row over it.

Row 5: Sl 1, k1, p1, k3, k2tog, yo, k4, p1, k2.

Row 7: Sl 1, k1, p1, k2, k2tog, yo, k5, p1, k2.

Row 9: Sl 1, k1, p1, k1, k2tog, yo, k6, p1, k2.

Row 11: Sl 1, k1, p1, ssk, yo, k7, p1, k2.

Row 13: Sl 1, k1, p1, k2, yo, ssk, k5, p1, M1, k1, [yo] 2 times, sl 1, pick up and knit sl st at beg of Row 10, psso—18 sts.

Row 14: Sl 1 wyif, [k1, p1] 3 times in "[yo] 2 times," p1, k2, p9, k3—22 sts.

Row 15: Sl 1, k1, p1, k3, yo, ssk, k4, p1, k1, sl 1, k6, sl 1, pick up and knit sl st at beg of Row 8, psso.

Row 16: Sl 1 wyif, p7, k2, p9, k3.

Row 17: Sl 1, k1, p1, k4, yo, ssk, k3, p1, k1, sl 1, [k1, yo] 5 times, k1, sl 1, pick up and knit sl st at beg of Row 6, psso—27 sts.

Row 18: Sl 1 wyif, p12, k2, p9, k3.

Row 19: Sl 1, k1, p1, k5, yo, ssk, k2, p1, k1, sl 1, [yo, k2tog] 5 times, yo, k1, sl 1, pick up and knit sl st at beg of Row 4, psso.

Row 20: Sl 1 wyif, p13, k2, p9, k3.

Row 21: Sl 1, k1, p1, k6, yo, ssk, k1, p1, k1, sl 1, [k1, yo] 11 times, k1, sl 1, pick up and knit sl st at beg of Row 2, psso—39 sts.

Row 22: Sl 1 wyif, p24, k2, p9, k3.

Row 23: Sl 1, k1, p1, k7, yo, k2tog, p1, k1, sl 1, k23, sl 1, pick up and knit sl st at beg of set-up row (or end of BO), psso.

Row 24: Sl 1, BO 24 sts, k2, p9, k3—15 sts.

Rep Rows 1–24 for desired length. Change color after each 24-row repeat, if desired.

Cart Wheels

(Work as for Boxcars, omitting first 15 sts.)

Note: The CO edge is at the right side of the photo.

CO 3 sts.

Hint: Mark the first sl st on the Set-up row and Rows 2, 4, 6, 8, and 10.

Set-up row: (WS) Sl 1, k2.

Rows 1, 3, 5, 7, 9, and 11: P1, k2.

Rows 2, 4, 6, 8, 10, and 12: Sl 1, k2.

Row 13: P1, M1, k1, [yo] 2 times, sl 1, pick up and knit sl st at beg of Row 10, psso—6 sts.

Row 14: Sl 1 wyif, ([k1, p1] 3 times) in "[yo] 2 times," p1, k2—10 sts.

Row 15: P1, k1, sl 1, k6, sl 1, pick up and knit sl st at beg of Row 8, psso.

Row 16: Sl 1 wyif, p7, k2.

Row 17: P1, k1, sl 1, [k1, yo] 5 times, k1, sl 1, pick up and knit sl st at beg of Row 6, psso—15 sts.

Row 18: Sl 1 wyif, p12, k2.

Row 19: P1, k1, sl 1, [yo, k2tog] 5 times, yo, k1, sl 1, pick up and knit sl st at beg of Row 4, psso—16 sts.

Row 20: Sl 1 wyif, p13, k2.

Row 21: P1, k1, sl 1, [k1, yo] 11 times, k1, sl 1, pick up and knit sl st at beg of Row 2, psso—27 sts.

Row 22: Sl 1 wyif, p24, k2.

Row 23: P1, k1, sl 1, k23, sl 1, pick up and knit sl st at beg of Set-up row, psso.

Row 24: Sl 1, BO 24 sts, k2.

Rep Rows 1–24 for desired length.

Beauty and the Bead

Note: The CO edge is at the left side of the photo. See pages 262–263 for instructions on knitting with beads.

String 6 beads for each 12-row pattern repeat.

SB1: Slip 1 bead next to left needle.

CO 9 sts.

Row 1: (RS) SB1, yo, k2tog, yo, k1, yo, ssk, k4—10 sts.

Row 2: P5, k5.

Row 3: SB1, yo, k2tog, yo, k3, yo, ssk, k3—11 sts.

Row 4: P4, k7.

Row 5: SB1, yo, k2tog, yo, k2, ssk, k1, yo, ssk, k2.

Row 6: P3, k1, ssk, [yo] 3 times, k2tog, k3—12 sts.

Row 7: SB1, yo, k2tog, yo, ssk, p1, k1, p1, k2tog, yo, k3.

Row 8: P4, k5, k2tog, k1—11 sts.

Row 9: SB1, yo, k2tog, yo, ssk, k1, k2tog, yo, k4.

Row 10: P5, k3, k2tog, k1—10 sts.

Row 11: SB1, yo, k2tog, yo, sl 2tog kwise, k1, p2sso, yo, k5.

Row 12: P6, k1, k2tog, k1—9 sts.

Rep Rows 1–12 for desired length.

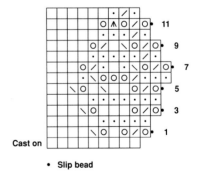

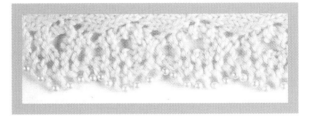

Cast on

• Slip bead

Joanie's Jubilee

Note: The CO edge is at the left side of the photo.

CO 22 sts.

Row 1: (RS) Sl 1, k1, yo, k2tog, [p2, k2] 3 times, p1, M1, work 5 sts in seed st—23 sts.

Rows 2 and 18: Seed 6, k1, [p2, k2] 3 times, k1, yo, k2tog, k1.

Row 3: Sl 1, k1, yo, k2tog, [p2, k2] 3 times, p1, M1, seed 6—24 sts.

Rows 4 and 16: Seed 7, k1, [p2, k2] 3 times, k1, yo, k2tog, k1.

Row 5: Sl 1, k1, yo, k2tog, [p2, k2] 3 times, p1, M1, seed 7—25 sts.

Rows 6 and 14: Seed 8, k1, [p2, k2] 3 times, k1, yo, k2tog, k1.

Row 7: Sl 1, k1, yo, k2tog, [p2, k2] 3 times, p1, M1, seed 8—26 sts.

Rows 8 and 12: Seed 9, k1, [p2, k2] 3 times, k1, yo, k2tog, k1.

Row 9: Sl 1, k1, yo, k2tog, [p2, k2] 3 times, p1, M1, seed 9—27 sts.

Row 10: Seed 10, k1, yf, wrap yarn clockwise around rem 16 sts on left needle 3 times (page 264), then [p2, k2] 3 times, k1, yo, k2tog, k1 over rem sts.

Row 11: Sl 1, k1, yo, k2tog, [p2, k2] 3 times, p1, k2tog, seed 8—26 sts.

Row 13: Sl 1, k1, yo, k2tog, [p2, k2] 3 times, p1, k2tog, seed 7—25 sts.

Row 15: Sl 1, k1, yo, k2tog, [p2, k2] 3 times, p1, k2tog, seed 6—24 sts.

Row 17: Sl 1, k1, yo, k2tog, [p2, k2] 3 times, p1, k2tog, seed 5—23 sts.

Row 19: Sl 1, k1, yo, k2tog, [p2, k2] 3 times, p1, k2tog, seed 4—22 sts.

Row 20: Seed 5, k1, [p2, k2] 3 times, k1, yo, k2tog, k1.

Rep Rows 1–20 for desired length.

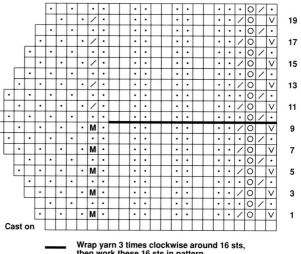

Cast on

—— Wrap yarn 3 times clockwise around 16 sts, then work these 16 sts in pattern.

Leaf Edging

Note: The CO edge is at the right side of the photo.

CO 8 sts.

Row 1: (RS) K5, yo, k1, yo, k2—10 sts.

Row 2: P6, k1f&b, k3—11 sts.

Row 3: K4, p1, k2, yo, k1, yo, k3—13 sts.

Row 4: P8, k1f&b, k4—14 sts.

Row 5: K4, p2, k3, yo, k1, yo, k4—16 sts.

Row 6: P10, k1f&b, k5—17 sts.

Row 7: K4, p3, k4, yo, k1, yo, k5—19 sts.

Row 8: P12, k1f&b, k6—20 sts.

Row 9: K4, p4, ssk, k7, k2tog, k1—18 sts.

Row 10: P10, k1f&b, k7—19 sts.

Row 11: K4, p5, ssk, k5, k2tog, k1—17 sts.

Row 12: P8, k1f&b, k2, p1, k5—18 sts.

Row 13: K4, p1, k1, p4, ssk, k3, k2tog, k1—16 sts.

Row 14: P6, k1f&b, k3, p1, k5—17 sts.

Row 15: K4, p1, k1, p5, ssk, k1, k2tog, k1—15 sts.

Row 16: P4, k1f&b, k4, p1, k5—16 sts.

Row 17: K4, p1, k1, p6, sl 1, k2tog, psso, k1—14 sts.

Row 18: P2tog, BO 5 sts, p3, k4—8 sts.

Rep Rows 1–18 for desired length.

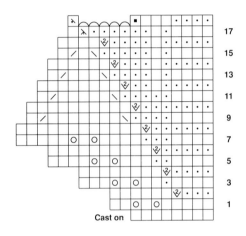

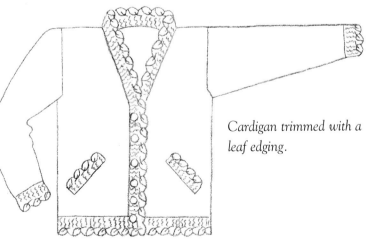

Cardigan trimmed with a leaf edging.

Duster Scallops

Note: The CO edge is at the left side of the photo.

CO 16 sts. Knit 1 row.

Row 1: YO, k2tog, k1, yo, k10, yo, k2tog, k1—17 sts.

Row 2 and all even-numbered rows: K2, yo, k2tog, knit to last st, p1.

Row 3: YO, k2tog, k1, yo, k2tog, yo, k9, yo, k2tog, k1—18 sts.

Row 5: YO, k2tog, k1, [yo, k2tog] 2 times, yo, k8, yo, k2tog, k1—19 sts.

Row 7: YO, k2tog, k1, [yo, k2tog] 3 times, yo, k7, yo, k2tog, k1—20 sts.

Row 9: YO, k2tog, k1, [yo, k2tog] 4 times, yo, k6, yo, k2tog, k1—21 sts.

Row 11: YO, k2tog, k1, [yo, k2tog] 5 times, yo, k5, yo, k2tog, k1—22 sts.

Row 13: YO, k2tog, k1, [yo, k2tog] 6 times, yo, k4, yo, k2tog, k1—23 sts.

Row 15: YO, k2tog, k1, [yo, k2tog] 7 times, yo, k3, yo, k2tog, k1—24 sts.

Row 17: YO, [k2tog] 2 times, [yo, k2tog] 7 times, k3, yo, k2tog, k1—23 sts.

Row 19: YO, [k2tog] 2 times, [yo, k2tog] 6 times, k4, yo, k2tog, k1—22 sts.

Row 21: YO, [k2tog] 2 times, [yo, k2tog] 5 times, k5, yo, k2tog, k1—21 sts.

Row 23: YO, [k2tog] 2 times, [yo, k2tog] 4 times, k6, yo, k2tog, k1—20 sts.

Row 25: YO, [k2tog] 2 times, [yo, k2tog] 3 times, k7, yo, k2tog, k1—19 sts.

Row 27: YO, [k2tog] 2 times, [yo, k2tog] 2 times, k8, yo, k2tog, k1—18 sts.

Row 29: YO, [k2tog] 2 times, yo, k2tog, k9, yo, k2tog, k1—17 sts.

Row 31: YO, [k2tog] 2 times, k10, yo, k2tog, k1—16 sts.

Row 32: K2, yo, k2tog, k11, p1.

Rep Rows 1–32 for desired length.

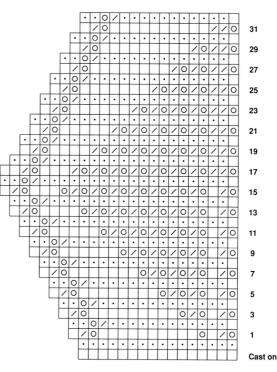

Horizontal

Remember to figure the width first for horizontally knitted borders. They can be bound off and sewn on later or continued into the pattern stitch of the garment body or piece.

Bobble-Stitch Garter Edging

(multiple of 6 sts + 5)

Bobble (MB): ([K1f&b] 2 times, k1) in same st, turn, k5, turn, p5, turn, k5, turn, sl 2nd, 3rd, 4th, and 5th st over 1st st, k1.

Row 1: (WS) Knit.

Row 2: K2, *MB, k5; rep from * end last rep k2.

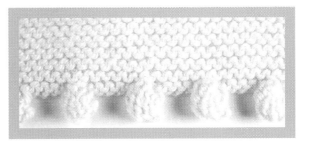

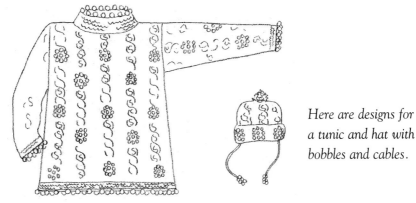

Here are designs for a tunic and hat with bobbles and cables.

Seed-Stitch Bobble Edging

(multiple of 4 sts + 3)

Set-up Row: (WS) Beg with k1, work 3 sts in seed st, *([p1, yo] 2 times, p1) in same st, turn, k5, turn, p5, turn, k2tog, k1, k2tog, turn, p3tog, seed 3; rep from *.

Work seed st for desired length.

Note: This edging can be worked along a vertical edge by working a bobble as above on the edge st every 4th row.

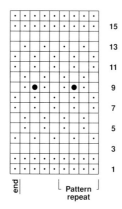

Puff Point Bobbles

(multiple of 10 sts + 1)

Bobble (MB): ([K1, p1] 2 times) in same st, [turn, k4] 3 times, turn, lift 2nd, 3rd, and 4th st over 1st st, k1.

Row 1: (RS) With A, *p5, MB, p4; rep from *, end last rep p5.

Rows 2, 4, 6, and 8: (WS) Purl.

Row 3: *P1, yo, p2, ssp, k1, p2tog, p2, yo; rep from *, end p1.

Row 5: *P2, yo, p1, ssp, k1, p2tog, p1, yo, p1; rep from *, end last rep p2.

Row 7: *P3, yo, ssp, k1, p2tog, yo, p2; rep from *, end last rep p3.

Row 9: *P5, k1, p4; rep from *, end last rep p5.

Rows 10 and 11: With B, purl.

Rows 12 and 13: With C, purl.

Double Seed and Bobble Edging

(multiple of 4 sts + 5)

Bobble (MB): ([k1, yo] 2 times, k1) in same st, turn, k5, turn, p5, turn, k5, turn, sl 2nd, 3rd, 4th, and 5th st over the 1st st, k1.

Row 1: (WS) Purl.

Rows 2 and 3: Knit.

Rows 4, 5, 12, and 13: *K1, p1, rep from *, end k1.

Rows 6, 8, 10, and 12: Knit the knits and purl the purls.

Rows 7 and 11: *P1, k1; rep from *, end p1.

Row 9: *K1, p1, MB, p1; rep from *, end k1.

Rows 14 and 15: Purl.

Row 16: BO in knit.

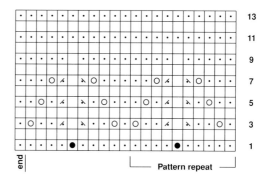

Double Bobble; Horizontal and Vertical

(multiple of 4 sts + 5)

Bobble (MB): ([k1f&b] 2 times, k1) in same st, [turn, p5, turn, k5] 2 times, sl 2nd, 3rd, 4th, and 5th st over 1st st, k1.

Rows 1 and 2: Knit.

Rows 3 and 7: (RS) K2, *MB, k3; rep from *, end MB, k2.

Rows 4, 6, 8, 10, 12, and 14: K2, purl to last 2 sts, k2.

Rows 5, 9, and 13: Knit.

Row 11: K2, MB, k3, MB, knit to last 2 sts, k2.

Rep Rows 11–14 for desired length.

Wrapped Shell

(multiple of 8 sts + 1)

Note: Slip all sts pwise.

Row 1: (WS) P1, sl 1 wyif, *p5, sl 3 wyif; rep from *, end last rep sl 1 wyif, p1.

Row 2: K1, sl 1 wyib, *k5 and sl onto cn, wrap yarn clockwise around these 5 sts (page 264) 6 times, sl the 5 sts back to right needle, sl 3 wyib; rep from *, end last rep sl 1 wyib, k1.

Row 3: P1, sl 1 wyif, *p4, insert right needle pwise into the next st and under the 2 sl strands from the 2 rows below, purl this group tog, sl 3 wyif; rep from *, end last rep sl 1 wyif, p1.

Row 4: Purl.

Embroider with duplicate st (page 189), if desired.

Wrapped Shell II

(multiple of 10 sts + 1)

Note: Slip all sts pwise.

Row 1: (WS) P1, sl 2 wyif, *p5, sl 5 wyif; rep from *, end p5, sl 2 wyif, p1.

Row 2: K1, sl 2 wyib, *k5 and slip onto cn; wrap yarn clockwise around these 5 sts (page 264) 8 times, sl the 5 sts back to right needle, sl 5 wyib; rep from *, end last rep sl 2 wyib, k1.

Row 3: P1, sl 2 wyif, *p4, insert right needle pwise into the next st and under the 2 sl strands from the 2 rows below, purl this group tog, sl 5 wyif; rep from *, end last rep sl 2 wyif, p1.

Row 4: Knit, dec 1 st.

Rows 5 and 7: *K5, p5; rep from *.

Rows 6, 8, 10, and 12: Knit the knits and purl the purls.

Rows 9 and 11: *P5, k5; rep from *.

Knotted Cord Edging

CO 8 sts.

Beg with a knit row, work 26 rows in St st. Break yarn and place sts on a holder. Make desired number of strips in the same manner. (Each knot requires 2 strips.)

Slip all strips onto left needle with right sides facing you. Working on first 2 strips only and keeping right sides facing at all times, cross first strip in front of second strip, then bring CO edge of second strip up in front of first strip and tuck it between the 2 strips and behind the first. Work first 8 garter sts of patt across sts of first strip and at the same time, catch in every other CO st of second strip. Next tuck rem CO edge of first strip behind sts of second strip and work the next 8 garter sts of patt across these sts, catching in every other CO st of first strip, thus completing the knot. Work rem knots in the same manner, continuing patt.

Note: Strips can be made with contrasting colors.

Knight's Edging

CO 6 sts.

Rows 1, 2 and 3: Work in seed st.

Rows 4 and 8: CO 3 sts, work to end in established seed st—9 sts.

Rows 5, 6, 7, 9, 10, 11, 12, 13, 14, and 15: Work in seed st.

Rows 16 and 20: BO 3 sts, work to end in seed st—6 sts.

Rows 17, 18, 19: Cont in seed st.

Rep Rows 1–20 for desired length.

Serf's Edging

Note: Each square is worked separately.

CO 9 sts.

Rows 1–10: Work in seed st. Break yarn and leave sts on needle—this forms one square. On the same needle, CO 9 sts and work Rows 1–10. Cont in this way until there are desired number of squares on needle. Do not break yarn after last square, but CO 2 sts, turn and knit across all squares on needle, CO 1 st bet each square and 2 sts at end of row.

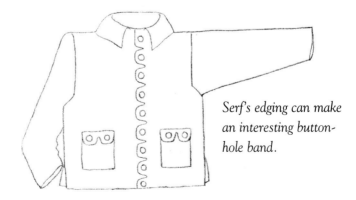

Serf's edging can make an interesting button-hole band.

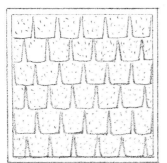

Shingles

(multiple of 7 sts)

Note: Each shingle is worked separately.
CO 7 sts.

Rows 1–10: Work in seed st. Break yarn, but leave sts on needle—this forms 1 shingle. Make as many shingles as desired. Work 10 rows St st. CO 4 sts and work Rows 1–10 for half shingles, making as many as there are full shingles, and placing sts on spare needle. Place spare needle with half shingles in front of needle with full shingles, then k2tog (1 st from each needle) across row. Rep for desired length, staggering shingles on each subsequent placement.

Pillow with shingles and knit cord edging.

Circles with Rhinestones

Circles: With B, CO 5 sts. Work in garter st, *inc 1 st at beg of each row until there are 11 sts. Work 6 rows even. Dec 1 st beg of each row until 5 sts rem, leaving sts on needle. Cut yarn. On same needle, CO 5 sts and rep from *. Make as many circles as needed for the design.

Header: With A, *CO 5 sts, k5 sts of circle; rep from *, end CO 5 sts.

Cont in desired patt. Sew rhinestones to center of each circle.

Diamond Drops

(multiple of 10 sts + 1)

Garter strip: CO desired number of sts. Work garter st for 1" (2.5 cm). BO all sts.

Diamonds: *CO 2 sts.

Row 1: K2.

Rows 2–10: YO, knit to end—11 sts after Row 10.

Rows 11–19: K2tog, knit to end—1 st after Row 19. Place st on holder. Rep from * for desired number of diamonds. Sew rem st of first diamond to 6th st of RS of garter strip, and each successive 10th st. With CC, embroider daisy st (page 202) and a French knot (page 203) in center of each diamond. Work French knots in center of garter strip.

Link Ladder Edging

Note: CO edge is at right side of photo
CO 3 sts.

Row 1 (WS): Purl.

Row 2: K1, M1, knit to last st, M1, k1—5 sts.

Rows 3–8: Rep last 2 rows—11 sts.

Row 9: Purl.

Row 10: Ssk, knit to last 2 sts, k2tog.

Rows 11–16: Rep last 2 rows—3 sts.

Rep from Row 1 for desired length.

Bottom Border: CO 5 sts, *pick up 1 st on side point of next diamond, CO 11 sts; rep from *, end k5. Knit 4 rows. BO all sts.

Top Border: Work as for bottom border.

Knotted Ladder

(multiple of 16 sts + 5)

Rows 1–8: Knit.

Rows 9–15: *BO 5, k3; rep from * end k5, turn.
BO 5, **k3, leave rem sts on needle. With spare
needle continue in garter st on 3 sts for 22 more
rows. Break yarn and leave 3 sts on holder.
Return to original needle; rep from **. Tie overhand knot in adjoining garter strips.

Next row: *CO 5 sts, k3 from holder; rep from *,
end CO 5 sts. Cont in garter st for 9 more rows.
BO all sts or cont in desired pattern.

Window Panes

(multiple of 10 sts + 5)

Rows 1–8: Knit.

Rows 9–15: *K5, leave rem sts on needle. With
spare needle cont in garter st for 6 more rows.
Break yarn and leave sts on holder. Return to original needle and BO 5 sts; rep from * to last 5 sts,
end knit last 5 sts for 8 rows but do not break
yarn. **CO 5 sts, k5; rep from **, end k5. Cont
in garter st for 8 more rows. BO all sts or cont in
desired pattern. Weave ribbon or fabric strip
through holes, if desired.

Folded Hem

CO desired number of sts. Work St st for 1½" (3.8 cm), ending with a RS row. Knit 1 (WS) row. Cont in desired patt st. Fold hem to inside along garter ridge. Sew in place.

Garter-Stitch Color Blocks
(multiple of 7 sts)

CO desired number of sts. *K7, change color; rep from *. Cont color sequence in the intarsia method, work garter st for 12 rows (6 ridges). Cont in desired patt st.

Cords

Knit cord (also called knitted cord, I-cord or French cord) is one of my favorite techniques, one with unlimited possibilities. Like many children, I learned to make knit cord using a wooden spool with nails hammered into it. One Christmas, I awoke to find "My Little Red Spinning Wheel"—a toy made by Mattel that could crank out yards and yards of knit cord. I made knit cord rugs, pot-holders, and hats.

Since then I've experimented a lot with knit cord and use it for adorning edges and borders, making decorative closures and buttons, and for applied cables and motifs. Use it when you can't find a button or closure to match a certain yarn, to complete a design, and for free-form embellishment.

For some knitters, knitting cord is therapy and they enjoy making yards of it. If you are not one of those knitters but want yards of knit cord for a project, try one of the following mechanical aids.

Knitting machines usually include instructions on how to make knit cord.

Knit cord gadgets, available from several companies (Bond, Hobby-Knit, Inox, Lion Brand), are designed specifically for making knit cord.

Wooden spools with four (or more) nails hammered into the top require a crochet hook. They are fun and easy to use, but not as quick as knitting.

Knit cord is a tube made with two double-pointed needles. The tube forms as the main yarn is pulled across the back of each row. Knit cord can be made separately and sewn to a knitted piece, or worked as part of the pattern stitch.

Stockinette stitch

CO 3 (or more) sts. *K3 (or more) sts. Do not turn work. Slide sts to right end of needle. Pull yarn to tighten. Rep from * for desired length.

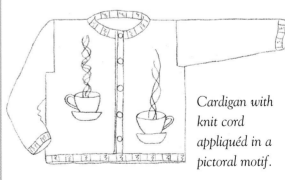

Cardigan with knit cord appliquéd in a pictoral motif.

Reverse stockinette stitch

CO 3 (or more) sts. *P3 (or more) sts. Do not turn work. Slide sts to right end of needle. Pull yarn to tighten. Rep from * for desired length.

Seed stitch

CO 5 sts. *K1, [p1, k1] 2 times. Do not turn work. Slide sts to right end of needle. Pull yarn to tighten. P1, [k1, p1] 2 times. Rep from * for desired length.

Multicolored

With A, CO 5 sts.
Row 1: *K5. Do not turn work. Slide sts to right end of needle.
Row 2: Join B and rep Row 1.
Row 3: Join C and rep Row 1. Draw next color to be used under the other 2 colors. Pull yarn to tighten.
Rep Rows 1–3 for desired length.

Tube Stitch

CO 5 sts.

Row 1: (RS) K1, [sl 1 pwise, k1] 2 times.

Row 2: Sl 1 pwise, [p1, sl 1 pwise] 2 times.

Rep Rows 1 and 2 for desired length.

Tunic with tube stitch appliqué.

Tunic with tube stitch appliquéd in an intertwining pattern.

Tube Stitch with Bobble

Bobble (MB): ([K1f&b] 2 times, k1) in same st—5 sts, turn. [P5, turn, k5, turn] 2 times. With left needle, pass 2nd, 3rd, 4th, and 5th st over the 1st st—1 st.

CO 5 sts.

Rows 1, 3, and 5: (RS) K1, [sl 1 pwise, k1] 2 times.

Rows 2, 4, 6, and 8: Sl 1 pwise, [p1, sl 1 pwise] 2 times.

Row 7: K1, sl 1 pwise, MB, sl 1 pwise, k1.

Rep Rows 1–8 for desired length.

Cable Cord

CO 5 sts.
Rows 1–4: Work St st knit cord (page 149).
Row 5: K1, 1/2LC, k1.
Rep Rows 1–5 for desired length.

Stockinette-Stitch Bobble Rope

(multiple of 2 sts + 1)

Bobble (MB): ([K1f&b] 2 times, k1) in same st—
5 sts, turn, [p5, turn, k5, turn] 2 times, p5, turn,
k5tog—1 st.
Row 1: (RS) Knit.
Row 2: *K1, MB; rep from *, end k1.
Row 3: BO all sts pwise.

Reverse Stockinette-Stitch Bobble Rope

(multiple of 4 sts + 3)

Bobble (MB): ([K1f&b] 2 times) in same st—4
sts, turn, k4, turn, p4, pass 2nd, 3rd, and 4th st
over the 1st st—1 st.

Row 1: Knit.
Row 2: *P3, MB; rep from *, end p3.
Row 3: BO all sts pwise.

Tube Stitch with Tassel

Work tube st (page 151) desired length, then make a tassel (page 22) and attach it to the cord.

Braided Cord with Tassel

Make three knit cords 1½ times the desired finished length and braid them. Leave ends unbraided and wrap with yarn to form tassel.

Two-Color Braided Cord

Make three knit cords 1½ times the desired finished length. Use two cords of one color and one of another. Braid.

Twisted Knit Cord

Make knit cord twice the desired length and folded in half. Anchor the fold securely and twist each end in the same direction until it kinks. Put both ends in one hand then release them, allowing them to twist around each other.

Knit Cord Bow

Make one knit cord the desired length and tie in a bow. Make a smaller cord and wrap around the center. Sew in place.

Hat with knit cord bows.

Knit Cord Button

Make knit cord the desired length and knot once (or twice for a larger button).

Straight Cord Edging

Make one knit cord the desired length and sew to the edge of a knitted piece. This makes a nice pocket edge.

Twisted Cord Edging

Make two knit cords, each the desired length. Twist them around each other and sew to the edge of a knitted piece.

Stacked Cords

Make any number of knit cords the desired length and sew side by side to a knitted piece.

Picot Cord

Make knit cord the desired length. Starting at lower edge, anchor knit cord in place and make a ¾" (2-cm) loop. *Sew cord in place straight for ¼" (6 mm), then make another ¾" (2-cm) loop. Rep from *.

Scribble Cord

Make knit cord the desired length, form into a series of loops. Sew in place, catching center sts at base of cord to secure.

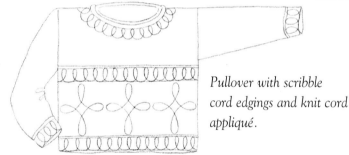

Pullover with scribble cord edgings and knit cord appliqué.

Button Loops

Make knit cord the desired length. Sew in place, forming a 1" (2.5 cm) loop for each button.

Knit and Applied Button Loop

Using the provisional method (page 259), CO 5 sts and work knit cord for desired length of button loop. Leave sts on needle. On same needle, pick up 5 sts from CO edge—10 sts. Work for desired length of button tab (shown in seed st).

2x4 Rib with Knotted Knit Cord

CO 4 sts.

Work knit cord for desired length. Then [k2tog] 2 times—2 sts. Sl sts onto spare needle. Rep for desired number of lengths, each time placing rem sts on same needle.

Row 1: With another needle, CO 4 sts, *k2 cord sts, CO 4 sts; rep from *.

Row 2: Purl.

Row 3: P4, *k2, p4; rep from *.

Row 4: Knit the knits and purl the purls.

Rep Row 4 for desired length. Tie knot at base of each cord.

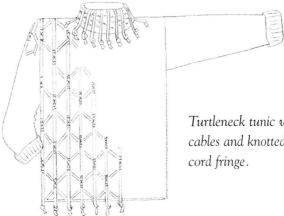

Turtleneck tunic with cables and knotted knit cord fringe.

Raindrops

CO 4 sts. Work knit cord for twice the desired length of raindrop. Do not BO. Rep for as many raindrops as desired. Slip all sts onto left needle.

Row 1: CO 5 sts, *k4 cord sts, CO 5 sts; rep from *.
Row 2: K5, *p4, k5; rep from *.
Row 3: Knit.

Rep Rows 2 and 3 for desired length. Bring CO edge of all cords behind k4 panel and sew in place.

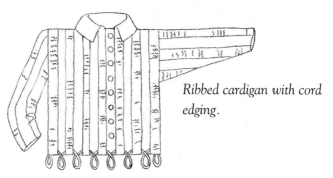

Ribbed cardigan with cord edging.

Looped Cord Edging

(multiple of 8 sts)

CO 4 sts. Work knit cord (page 149) for 4" (10 cm). Rep for desired number of cords, leaving sts on needle. K4 from 1st cord, *k4 from next cord on needle, bring CO edge of previous cord in back of cord just knit and pick up and knit the 4 CO sts; rep from *, end by picking up and knitting the 4 CO sts of last cord. Cont in desired pattern.

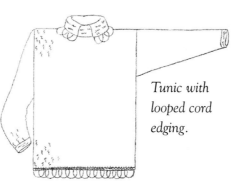

Tunic with looped cord edging.

Twisted Cord Edging

(multiple of 9 sts)

CO 3 sts. Work knit cord (page 149) for 4" (10 cm). Rep for desired number of cords, leaving sts on needle. K3tog from 1st cord, *k3tog from next cord on needle, CO 5 sts, twist these 2 cords tog, k3tog from CO edge of 2nd cord just worked, then k3tog from CO edge of 1st cord just worked, k3tog from next cord on needle; rep from *, end k3tog from CO edge of 2nd cord just worked, then k3tog from CO edge of 1st cord just worked.

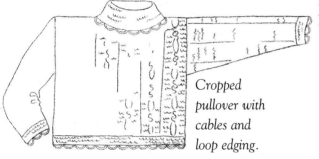

Cropped pullover with cables and loop edging.

Arbor Loop Trim

(multiple of 8 sts + 2)

Make desired number of 3" (7.5-cm) pieces of 4-st knit cord (page 149) and place both ends of each piece on a spare needle.

Row 1: (RS) CO 2 sts, *[k2tog] 2 times (the CO end of one cord), CO 2 sts, [k2tog] 2 times (the live sts of one cord), CO 2 sts; rep from *.

Row 2 and all even-numbered rows: Knit the knits and purl the purls.

Row 3: P2, *sl next 4 sts onto cn and hold in back, k2, sl the 2 purl sts from cn onto left needle and purl them, k2 from cn, p2; rep from *.

Rows 5, 7, 9, 11, 15, 17, and 19: P2, *k2, p2; rep from *.

Row 13: P2, k2, *p2, sl next 4 sts onto cn and hold in front, k2, sl the 2 purl sts from cn onto left needle and purl them, k2 from cn; rep from *, end p2, k2, p2.

Rep Rows 2–19 for desired length.

Torque Knot

(multiple of 8 sts + 2)

Make desired number of 3" (7.5-cm) pieces of 4-st knit cord (page 149) and place both ends of each piece on a spare needle.

Row 1: (RS) CO 2 sts, *[k2tog] 2 times (the CO end of one cord), CO 2 sts [k2tog] 2 times (the live sts of one cord), CO 2 sts; rep from *.

Rows 2, 4, 10, 12, 14, and 16: K2, *p2, k2; rep from *.

Row 3: P2, *k2, p2; rep from *.

Rows 5 and 17: P2, *sl 2 sts onto cn and hold in back, sl next 2 sts onto cn and hold in front, ssk the next 2 sts on left-hand needle, k2 sts on cn in front of work, k2tog the 2 sts on cn at back of work, p2; rep from *—mult of 6 sts + 2.

Rows 6 and 18: K2, *p4, k2; rep from *.

Rows 7 and 19: P2, *k4, p2; rep from *.

Rows 8 and 20: K2, *sl 1 st onto cn and hold in back of work, sl next 2 sts onto another cn and hold in front of work, p1f&b, k2 from cn held in front of work, p1f&b from cn held at back of work, p2; rep from *—mult of 8 sts + 2.

Rows 9, 11, 13, 15, and 21: P2, *k2, p2; rep from *.

BO in patt.

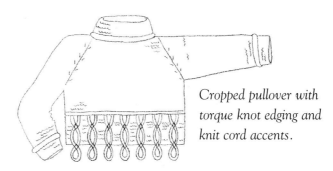

Cropped pullover with torque knot edging and knit cord accents.

Rosie's Rib

(multiple of 7 sts + 2)

With MC,

Row 1: P2, *k5, p2; rep from *.

Row 2: K2, *p5, k2; rep from *.

Rows 3–12: Rep Rows 1 and 2.

Row 13: Join CC. P2 with MC, *k2 with MC, change to CC, k1, yo, k1 in next st. Working on 3 CC sts only, work tube st (page 151) for 1¼" (3.2 cm), k3tog. Place st on holding thread, form knot in tube st, place rem st on right needle, with MC, k2, p2; rep from *.

Rows 14–17: Rep Rows 2 and 1. BO all sts.

Using a stem st (page 193), embroider stem and leaves at base of each knot. Using a straight st (page 192), embroider leaves around bud.

Chaplet Loop with Garter Ridges

CO 40 sts.

Rows 1 and 13: K37, yo, k2tog, k1.

Row 2: Sl 1, purl to end.

Rows 3 and 15: BO 28 sts, k8, yo, k2tog, k1—12 sts.

Rows 4, 8, and 16: Sl 1, k11.

Rows 5, 7, 9, 11, 17, 19, 21, and 23: K9, yo, k2tog, k1.

Rows 6 and 18: Sl 1, k2, p9.

Rows 10 and 14: Sl 1, k2, purl to end.

Row 12: Sl 1, k11, CO 28 sts—40 sts.

Row 20: Sl 1, k10, turn up the end of the narrow knitting and knit a loop of the first BO st of long strip tog with the last st on the needle.

Row 22: Sl 1, k2, p8, knit a loop of the last CO st of long strip tog with the last st on the needle.

Rep Rows 12–23 for desired length.

Chaplet Loop with Seed Stitch

CO 35 sts.

Set-up row: K1, p1; rep from *, end k1.

Row 1: (RS) Sl 1, yo, k2tog, work to end, knitting the purls and purling the knits (seed st).

Rows 2 and 14: BO 28 sts, seed 3, yo, k2tog, k2—8 sts.

Rows 3, 5, 7, 9, 15, and 17: Sl 1, yo, k2tog, k1, seed to end.

Rows 4, 6, 8, 10, 16, 18, 20, and 22: Seed 4, yo, k2tog, k2.

Row 11: Sl 1, yo, k2tog, k1, seed 4, CO 27 sts—35 sts.

Row 12: Seed 31, yo, k2tog, k2.

Row 13: Sl 1, yo, k2tog, k1, seed to end.

Row 19: Sl 1, k10, turn up the end of the narrow knitting and knit a loop of the first BO st of long strip tog with last st on needle.

Row 21: Sl 1, k2, p8, knit a loop of the last CO st of long strip tog with last st on needle.

Rep Rows 11–22 for desired length.

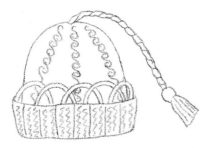

Cable cap with chaplet loops and cable knit cord with tassel.

Knit Cord Motifs

Knit cord can be used to create any motif imaginable, including mock cables and Celtic knots. It can be worked on any background, but is particularly easy to sew onto flat textures. Using foam board and pins, baste the cord to the background, then sew it either from the front or the back—whichever you prefer. If you want to join the live stitches from the needle with the cast-on stitches, use the Kitchener stitch (page 261) with an invisible cast-on (page 260), or cut the cord close to the cast-on edge and unravel to expose live stitches.

For best results when forming the cord into celtic knots or frogs, use T-pins to anchor (beginning with the cast-on edge) against a piece of Styrofoam board at least 10" (25.5 cm) square. Wrap the cord firmly around T-pins placed into the piece of Styrofoam, allowing for some contraction of the piece when the pins are removed.

Bell

Pine Tree

Cords

Decorative Leaf

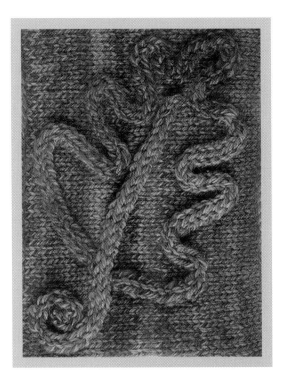

Flower

See page 35 for leaf instructions.

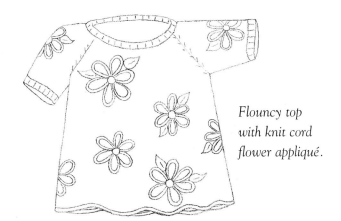

*Flouncy top
with knit cord
flower appliqué.*

Numbers

Alphabet

Snake

Body: CO any number of sts to make knit cord or tube st for desired length.

Head: Work back and forth in St st, inc 1 st each end of needle every RS row until piece measures ½" (1.3 cm). Then dec 1 st each end of needle every other row until 2 or 3 sts rem. *Next row:* Dec to 1 st. Fasten off. Sew on sequins, beads, or rhinestones, or use French knots (page 203) for snake's eyes. Use crochet chain (page 262) for tongue.

Cords

Candy Cane

Make two 8" (20.5-cm) long cords—one each of red and white. Twist the cords tog into cane shape.

Christmas Tree

CO 6 sts. Work k1, p1 rib for 1" (2.5 cm). K3 sts and place on holder. Work knit cord on last 3 sts for 11" (28 cm). Place sts on holder. Pick up first 3 sts from holder and work knit cord until piece measures 11" (28 cm). Use Kitchener st (page 261) to join tops of cords. Shape tree by pinning in place onto background over foam board. Sew in place. Decorate tree with embroidered straight stitches (page 192), French knots (page 203), and double cross-st (page 191).

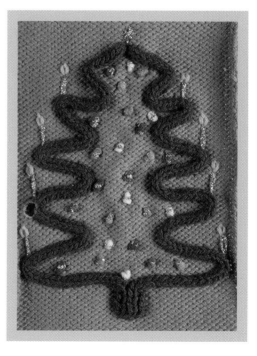

Pillow with appliquéd Christmas trees and trimmed with knit cord.

Anchor

Spiral

Side Winder

Make cord any size and length. Apply to background in a snake shape, as shown.

Cords

Open Twist Cable with Bars

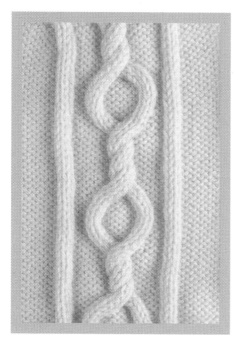

Diamond and Rope Cable

Double Wave

Quatrefoil

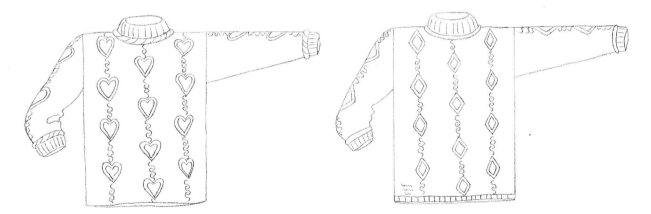

Two tunics with mock cable cord motifs and cord trim on necks and cuffs.

Cords

Corset Lace

Fiddlehead Fern

Celtic Stonework Knot

Work tube st (page 151) for desired length. Beg and end at top, work in "under, over" motions to form intertwined knot as shown. Join CO edge to BO edge with Kitchener st (page 261).

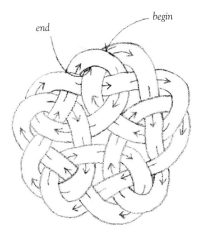

Celtic stonework pillow trimmed with knit cord and knitted tassels.

Celtic Connemara Knot

Work tube st (page 151) for desired
length. Beg and end at top, work in
"under, over" motions as shown.

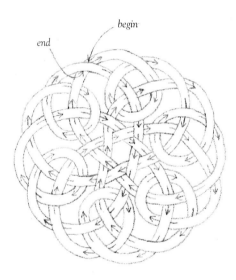

Celtic Interlacing Knot

Beg and end at lower right, work in "under, over" motions as shown.

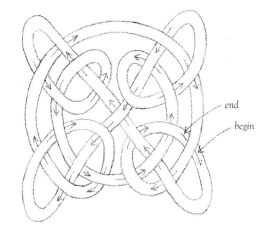

end

begin

Frogs and Closures

Making closures from knit cord in the garment yarn or a carefully chosen coordinating yarn gives a design a professional finish. It also eliminates the hassle of trying to find just the right buttons. To make cord or buttons firmer, stuff with piping cord (available at most fabric shops).

When making cord for frogs, do not bind off the stitches; leave them on a holder so length can be added or subtracted as needed. Form the frogs by using T-pins to anchor (beginning with the cast-on edge) against a piece of Styrofoam board at least 10" (25.5 cm) square.

Fishtail Frog/Button

Work as shown, pinning outer loop in place. Work each subsequent loop inside previous loop.

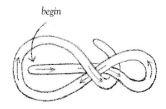
begin

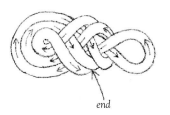
end

Spiral Loop

Beg at lower edge, wind cord into clockwise spiral, three loops (the 2nd forms the buttonhole), and end with another clockwise spiral.

end

begin

Cords

Celtic Knot Clover

Beg and end as shown, wrap cord
into three interlocking loops, then
pull on outer edges of the loops to
form clover shape.

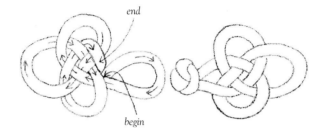

Figure-Eight

Beg at the center, wrap cord in a figure-eight.

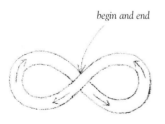

Royal Reverse Frog

Beg at upper right edge, form clock-wise spiral followed by three-sided loop to the left (for buttonhole), and end with a clockwise spiral at the lower right.

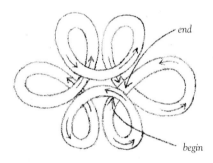

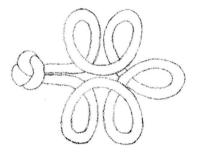

Palmate Frog

Use Kitchener st (page 261) to join the CO end to live sts for each of two cords. Shape each piece as shown, forming a loop buttonhole.

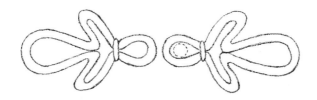

Hunter's Heart

This frog requires two cords. Shape shorter cord into figure eight, beg and end at crossover point. Beg at base of crossover, shape longer cord into clockwise spiral, loop it around the figure eight, and end with a clockwise spiral above the figure eight. Tie two other lengths of cord tog for button.

begin

Elongated Double Loop

Use Kitchener st (page 261) to join CO end to live sts to form a loop. Flatten loop as shown. Wrap yarn four times around each end to form buttonholes.

Hats with frogs.

Serpent

Use Kitchener st (page 261) to join CO end to live sts of cord. Loop cord around itself into a knot as shown.

Spiral

Fold cord in half. Form each end into spiral as shown. Tie another length of cord into a single knot for button.

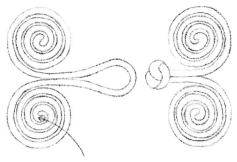

begin

Basketweave Knots

Working in a counterclockwise direction, shape cord into four interlocking loops as shown. Tie another length into a single knot for button.

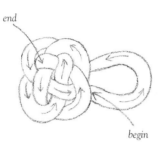

end

begin

Leaf Frog with Single Knot Button

Beg at the loop/button end, form cord into leaf shape as shown. Tie another length of cord into a single knot for button.

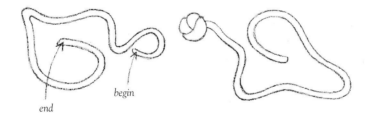

end   begin

Florette

Beg at center, wrap cord into counterclockwise spiral, then use a threaded needle to anchor rem cord into accordion shape. Form accordion around spiral. Tack in place. Tie another length of cord into a single knot for button.

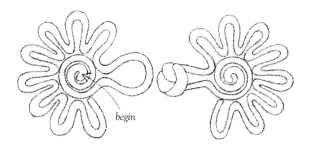

begin

Clover

Beg at center, form cord into four loops as shown. Tie another length of cord into a single knot for button.

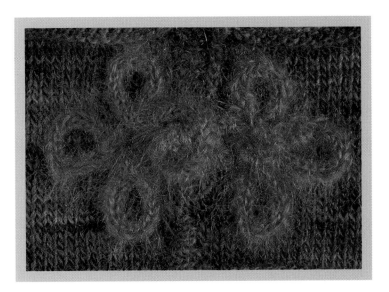

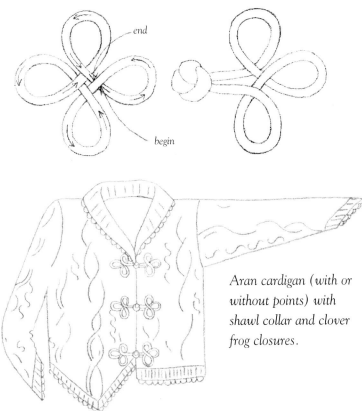

Aran cardigan (with or without points) with shawl collar and clover frog closures.

Quatrefoil

Beg and end as shown, form
cord into four counter-clockwise
loops. Tie cord into a double
knot for button.

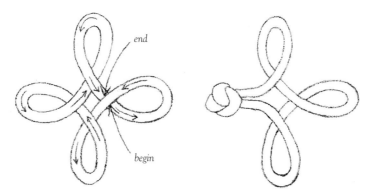

end

begin

Cord Ties

Cords can be picked up and knitted from a knitted background, or worked separately and sewn in place.

Regal Frog Tassel

Beg and end as shown, form cord into eight loops. Make a tassel (page 221) and attach to base.

begin　　　　*end*

Captain's Frog Tassel

Beg and end at center, make three clockwise loops as shown. Make a tassel (page 221) and secure to base of frog. Work a twisted cord (page 266) and tie around neck of tassel.

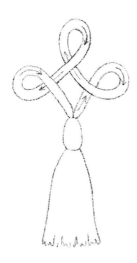

Embroidery

You can create beautiful, lavish "wearable art" by using embroidery stitches in yarn combinations. But beware. Once you get hooked on the technique, it will be very difficult to make a plain knitted piece. Embroidery is traditionally worked on fabric that has been pre-printed with a design or by counting threads. To keep embroidery even on a knitted background you'll need to count stitches and rows. You may also want a template or a cutout to help you place the design.

Embroidery stitches have to be laid and anchored carefully on the background. The bars between knit stitches are very useful for anchoring such embroidery stitches as French knots. Embroidery looks best on backgrounds with simple and flat stitch patterns such as stockinette, reverse stockinette, garter, seed, and basketweave. Avoid embroidering on heavy textured pattern stitches.

Cotton, silk, angora, ribbon, and wool can be purchased in small amounts and all work well on knitted backgrounds. Avoid novelty and bouclé yarns that have bumps and uneven strands, unless you use just a small amount for a specific look.

Use blunt tapestry needles for most embroidery on knitting, but if you use a yarn, such as silk, that requires extra anchoring and unravels easily, by all means use a pointed needle.

Following are popular embroidery stitches shown on a stockinette-stitch background, along with some creative combinations for inspiration.

Duplicate Stitch

Duplicate stitch, also called Swiss Darning, is exactly what its name implies—it duplicates a knitted stitch. You can work duplicate stitch in three directions—horizontally (the most common for covering large areas), vertically, and diagonally.

Horizontal: Bring threaded needle out from back to front at the base of the V of the knitted stitch you want to cover. *Working right to left, pass needle in and out under the stitch in the row above it and back into the base of the same stitch. Bring needle back out

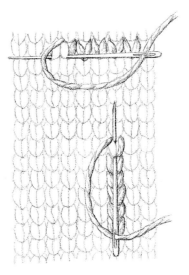

at the base of the V of the next stitch to the left. Repeat from *.

Vertical: Beginning at lowest point, work as for horizontal duplicate stitch, ending by bringing the needle back out at the base of the stitch directly above the stitch just worked.

Diagonal upward slanting: Beginning at lowest point, work as for horizontal duplicate stitch, ending by bringing the needle back out one stitch above and one stitch to the left or right of the stitch just worked.

Diagonal downward slanting: Beginning at uppermost point, work as for diagonal slanting upward duplicate stitch, ending by bringing the needle back out one stitch down and one stitch to the left or right of the stitch just worked.

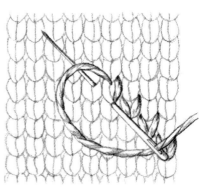

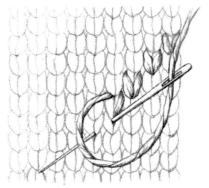
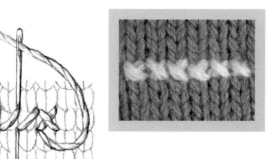

Cross-Stitch

Designs in cross-stitch are usually worked by following a chart and counting all stitches and rows. To avoid excess bulk, you may want to split your yarn into plies or use a lighter weight yarn than you used for the background. For the best appearance, the top strand of all cross-stitches should be worked in the same direction.

Bring threaded needle out from back to front at lower left edge of the knitted stitch you want to cover. Working left to right, *insert the needle at the upper right edge of the same stitch and bring it back out at the lower left edge of the adjacent stitch, directly below and in line with the insertion point. Repeat from * to form one half of the cross. Then work from right to left in the same manner to work the other half of the cross-stitch.

Double Cross-Stitch

Work cross-stitch as described above, then bring needle out at the base of the crossed yarn, over the cross, and back in at the top of the cross, then out again at the right side of the cross and back in on the left side. The double cross-stitch in the sample is worked over four knitted stitches.

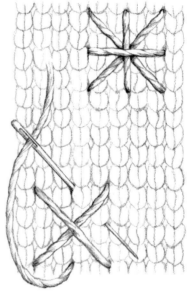

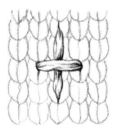

St. George Cross-Stitch

*Bring threaded needle out from back to front at the base of the knitted stitches you want to cover. Insert the needle in the stitch directly above two or more rows. Then work a horizontal stitch in the same manner across this vertical stitch.

Straight Stitch

Straight stitches can be worked side by side or radiating out from a center point. For best results, avoid stitches that are too long, too loose, or too close together.

*Bring threaded needle out from back to front at the base of the knitted stitch(es) you want to cover. Insert the needle at the top of the stitch(es) you want to cover. Repeat from *.

Long and Short Straight Stitches

Work straight stitches, alternating long stitches with short stitches.

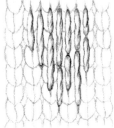

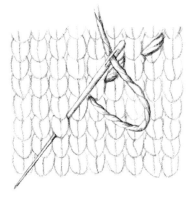

Running Stitch

Working small straight stitches (above), pass the threaded needle over one knitted stitch and under the next to form a dashed line. The stitches can be worked in equal or varying lengths, horizontally, vertically, or diagonally.

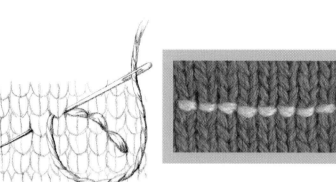

Back Stitch

Bring threaded needle out from back to front between the first two knitted stitches you want to cover. *Insert needle at the right edge of the right stitch and bring it back out at the left edge of the remaining stitch. Insert needle again between the first two stitches and bring it out between the next two to be covered. Repeat from *. The stitches can be worked in any direction.

Stem Stitch

This stitch is excellent for flower stems and outlines.

Bring threaded needle out from back to front at the center of a knitted stitch. *Insert the needle into the upper right edge of the next stitch to the right, and then out again at the center of the stitch below. Repeat from *, working regular, slightly slanted stitches.

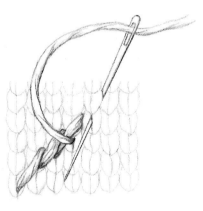

Holbein Stitch

This stitch is also called a double running stitch.

Work running stitch (page 192) from right to left over the knitted stitch(es) you want to cover, forming horizontal dashed lines. Then, working left to right, work vertical running stitches to connect the horizontal dashes.

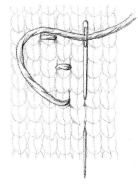

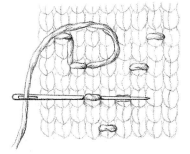

Chevron Stitch

This is worked in the same manner as cross-stitch (page 190).

Working from left to right, bring threaded needle out from back to front at the base of a knitted stitch. *Insert needle one stitch to the right and two rows up. Then bring needle out one stitch to the right and two rows down (even with where the needle came out the first time). Repeat from *, making a row of stitches that lean from left to right. Work from right to left in the same manner to form left-leaning stitches that complete the chevron.

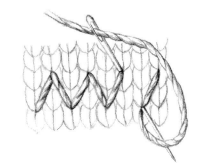

Fly Stitch

*Bring threaded needle out from back to front at the upper left corner of a knitted stitch. Insert needle at upper right corner of the same stitch forming a loop and back out at the center of the same stitch, holding the loop below the tip of the needle as it comes out. Insert needle into center of stitch directly below. Repeat from *.

To work a vertical grouping, bring needle out again at upper left corner of the stitch directly below the one just covered and work in the same manner. To work a horizontal grouping, bring needle out at upper left corner of the stitch to the right of the one just covered.

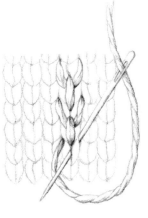

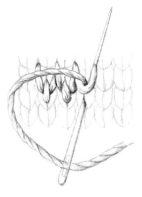

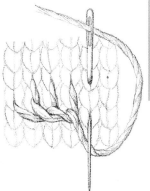

Blanket Stitch

This stitch, worked from left to right, is great for edging a knitted garment or blanket.

Bring threaded needle out from back to front at the center of a knitted stitch. *Insert needle at center of next stitch to the right and two rows up, and out at the center of the stitch two rows below. Repeat from *.

Chain Stitch

Bring threaded needle out from back to front at the center of a knitted stitch. *Form a short loop and insert needle back where it came out. Keeping the loop under the needle, bring the needle back out in the center of the next stitch to the right. Repeat from *.

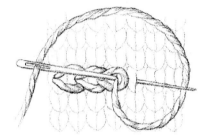

Crocheted Chain Stitch

This looks like the chain stitch (above), but is worked with a crochet hook through the knitted background.

Holding yarn under background, insert hook through the center of a knitted stitch, pull up a loop, *insert hook into center of next stitch to the right, pull a second loop up through the first loop on the hook. Repeat from *.

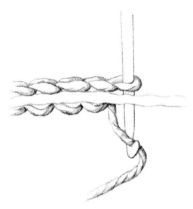

Chained Feather Stitch

This stitch is particularly suitable for a stockinette-stitch background because the parallel lines formed by the knitted stitches are easy to follow.

Bring threaded needle out from back to front at the upper left corner of a knitted stitch. *Form a short loop and insert needle back where it came out. Keeping the loop under the needle, bring the needle back out at the lower right corner of the stitch. Insert the needle at the lower right corner of the next stitch to the right, one row down, and back out at the upper left corner of the next stitch to the right. Form a short loop and insert needle back where it just came out. Keeping the loop under the needle, bring the needle back out at the lower left corner of the same stitch. Insert the needle at the lower left corner of the next stitch to the left and back out at the upper left corner of the next stitch to the left. Repeat from *.

Split Chain Stitch

This stitch is best worked with a yarn that splits easily.

Bring threaded needle out from back to front at the center of a knitted stitch. *Insert needle into center of a stitch one or two stitches to the right and one row up. Bring the needle back out in the stitch to the left, piercing the working thread. Repeat from *.

Seeded Stitch

Work tiny straight stitches (page 192) in all directions on the knitted background.

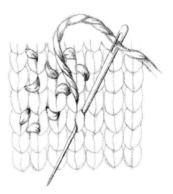

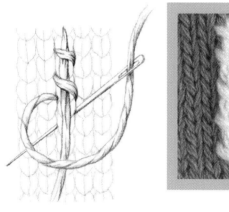

Couching Stitch

There are many ways to work couching; the simplest method is shown here.

Lay the thread (or threads) to be covered on top of the knitted background. Bring threaded needle out from back to front at the left side of this thread. *Bring the needle over this thread and insert it close to the right side of this thread. Bring the needle back out a short distance below, and repeat from *.

Couching with Cross-Stitch

This technique is similar to couching (above) but is worked with cross-stitches and forms a wider band.

Lay several strands of thread to be covered on top of the knitted background. Bring threaded needle out from back to front at the upper left edge of a stitch on the left side of this thread group. *Bring needle over the thread group and insert it into the lower right edge of the same stitch. Bring needle out at the lower left edge of the stitch, over the thread group, and back in at the upper right edge of the stitch, forming a cross. Bring the needle back out at the upper left edge of a stitch a few rows down and repeat from *.

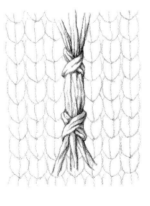

Jacobean Couching

This pretty stitch, also called cross-hatching, makes an attractive trellis or filler for the centers of flowers or other shapes where an open effect is desired.

Make long straight stitches (page 192) on a knitted background parallel to each other and about ½" (1.3 cm) apart. Work another series of straight stitches on top of and at right angles to the previous ones. Then couch the resulting crosses with tiny straight stitches (shown) or small cross stitches (page 190).

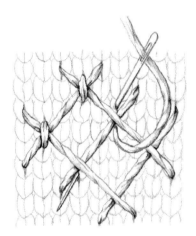

Angel Wings

Work a group of three or four long horizontal straight stitches (page 192) across several stitches on a knitted background. Then work one or two vertical straight stitches over one or two knitted stitches at the center of the horizontal stitches, pulling the threads together.

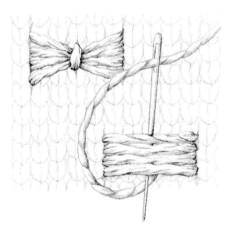

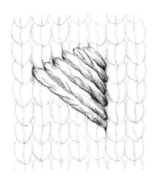

Satin Stitch

This stitch is ideal for filling in open areas, such as the center of leaves or flowers.

Work closely spaced straight stitches (page 192), in graduated lengths as desired, and entering and exiting in the center of or at the side of the knitted stitches.

Fishbone Stitch

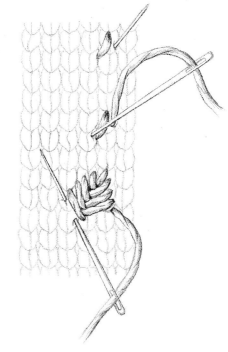

Made from straight stitches worked at obtuse angles to each other, this stitch forms a lovely leaf shape. It is worked from top to bottom.

Bring threaded needle out from back to front in the center of a knitted stitch, and then back in a short distance away. Working from right to left, *bring the needle out a short distance below where the previous stitch came out, and back in next to where the previous stitch went in, crossing over the lower tip of the stitch. Bring needle out to the right of and a short distance below the stitch just worked and back in to the right of and next to where that stitch went in, again crossing over the lower tip of the stitch. Repeat from *, keeping a strong slant to each stitch.

Leaf Stitch

This slanted stitch is worked like the fly stitch and forms a leaf shape with a central "vein."

Bring threaded needle out from back to front in the center of a knitted stitch. Make a diagonal straight stitch (page 192), inserting the needle a short distance down and to the right. *Bring needle out to the left of and just below the top of the straight stitch, insert it to the right of the straight stitch, and then back out at the base of the same stitch, holding the yarn below the tip of the needle as it comes out. Insert needle into center of stitch directly below the one just exited. Repeat from *, always working below previous stitches and keeping the stitches flat and strongly slanted.

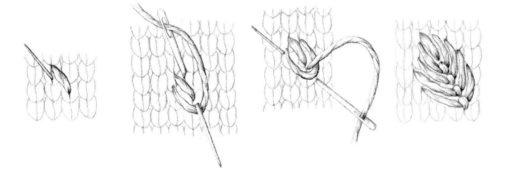

Fern Stitch

This stitch is made from three straight stitches of equal length that radiate from the same point. The center stitches of the three-stitch groups form a line.

Bring threaded needle out from back to front where you want the central point to be. *Working from left to right, make three straight stitches (page 192)

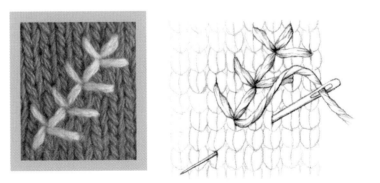

radiating from this point. After the third stitch, bring the needle back out below the grouping so that the center stitch of the next three-stitch group will be in line with that of the previous group. Repeat from *.

Daisy Stitch

This stitch, also called single or detached chain stitch, is formed from chain stitches. Each chain stitch forms a petal, and when grouped, the petals form a flower.

Beginning each stitch at the same point on the knitted background, work six chain stitches (page 196) to form a flower.

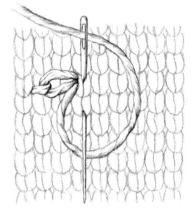

Double Daisy Stitch

Work five chain stitches as above, but make the stitches larger and work a second, smaller chain stitch in the center of each stitch.

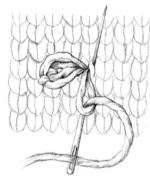

Decadent Daisy Stitch:

Work five chain stitches as above, then work straight stitches (page 192) in the center of and between each chain stitch. Work a French knot (below) in the center of the group.

French Knot

Work French knots singularly or in clusters to make flowers or flower centers.

Bring needle out of the knitted background from back to front, wrap yarn around needle one to three times and use your thumb to hold it in place as you pull needle through the wraps into the background a short distance (one background thread) from where the thread first emerged.

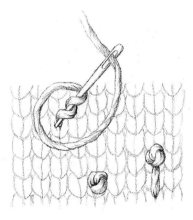

Stemmed French Knot

Work a straight stitch (page 192) that radiates out from a French knot.

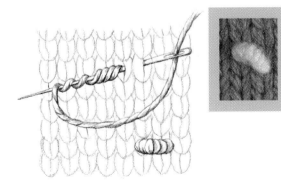

Bouillon Stitch

This stitch is also called worm stitch, rolled stitch, and Chinese rose.

Bring threaded needle out from back to front in the center of a knitted stitch. Leaving a long loop, insert the needle one stitch over, and bring it back out through the center of the initial stitch. Wrap the loop of thread around the needle as many times as desired, then insert the needle back into the same spot it entered before, and pull firmly.

Rosette Stitch

This stitch may be used alone or in clusters.

*Insert threaded needle in and out of the knitted background so that the distance between the entry and exit points are equal to the desired rosette diameter. Do not pull the needle through. Wrap the working thread three to five times around the needle, keeping it under the ends of the needle. Pull the needle through and insert it just below the exit point, making a small straight stitch to couch the wrapped thread at the bottom of the circle. Bring needle back out just below the wrapped threads and in line with the previous couching. Make a small straight stitch to couch the top half of the circle.

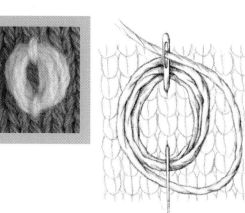

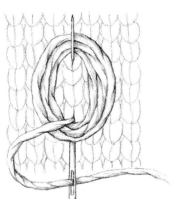

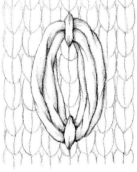

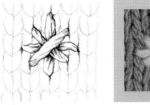

Star Stitch

This stitch can be used singly, as an all-over design, or as a border repeat.

Working all stitches the same size, make a cross-stitch (page 190) on top of a St. George cross-stitch (page 191).

Elongated Star

Work a cross-stitch (page 190) on top of an elongated St. George cross-stitch (page 191).

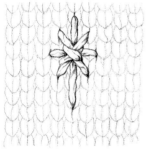

North Star

Work a small cross-stitch (page 190) in the center of an elongated star (above).

Woven Web

Make a foundation by working five straight stitches (page 192) of equal length radiating out from the same point on the knitted background. Weave the needle over and under the straight stitches until they are half covered.

Whip Stitch

Whip stitch forms a widely spaced overcast stitch.

Bring the threaded needle out from back to front at the center of a knitted stitch. Moving from left to right, *insert the needle over two knitted stitches and up two rows. Bring the needle back out through the center of the stitch two rows below. Repeat from *.

Combinations

The following swatches show interesting ways to combine embroidery stitches with each other or with knitted stitches. Keep in mind that the type of yarn you use for embroidery can greatly affect the overall appearance.

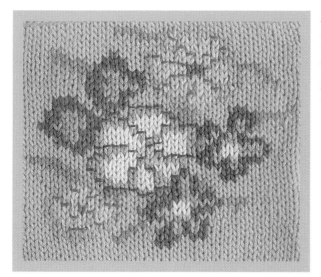

Floral Panel

Duplicate stitch and Holbein stitch are worked in embroidery floss on a stockinette-stitch background. The Holbein stitch is worked with just three strands of floss.

Single Flower

Duplicate stitch, stem stitch and large running stitches are worked on a stockinette-stitch background.

Indian Eagle

Duplicate stitch, stem stitch, fly stitch, and blanket stitch are worked on a stockinette-stitch background.

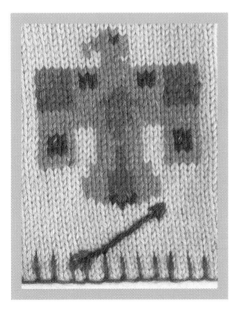

Whip Stitch and Blanket Stitch

Whip stitch is used for the diagonal seam and blanket stitch is used to hold the rolled hem in place.

Bell Border

Star stitch (in metallic) accentuates the bell-shaped pattern.

Diamond Daisy Cable

Although the flower looks knitted in here, it is actually embroidered daisy stitch, worked in brushed wool.

Cable Daisy Stitch

This is the same as the diamond daisy (above) but with a different cable.

Butterflies

Fly stitch is worked in silk ribbon and French knots are worked in variegated cotton floss on a stockinette-stitch background.

Fringes, Tassels, Pom-Poms, and Ties

Fringes

A fringe is a fringe is a fringe. Not so! Take a look at these fringing techniques—you may want to think about using one to give an existing piece a new look.

Traditionally, fringes are cut and applied with a crochet hook to the edge of a knitted piece. In addition, I've included some that are knitted lengthwise in one piece and partially unravelled to form fringe. Unravel more stitches for longer fringe, fewer for shorter fringe. Various stitches and multiple colors can be used. Different textured yarns and embellishments help create elegant fringes. Fringes may be left looped, cut, or knotted.

Some fringes are made by knitting loops into the background. You can vary the loop length by the number of times you wind the yarn around your finger, or by the number of fingers you wind the yarn around. Adjust the density of the loops by working more or fewer sts and rows between the loop stitches. Use flat or textured yarns; try yarns with long fibers, such as mohair, for a faux fur look.

Single Knot Fringe

Cut several strands of yarn (the more strands, the thicker the fringe) two times the desired fringe length, plus about 1" (2.5 cm) for knotting. Fold the yarn in half. Insert a crochet hook into the knitted piece, from back to front, catch the folded yarn, and pull it through the knitting. Draw the yarn ends through the loop and pull to tighten. Trim ends to even lengths. Note: Sample shows knit cord (page 149) sewn above fringe.

Double Knot Fringe

Work Single Knot Fringe (page 211) across edge of knitted piece. Working from left to right with RS of work facing, knot together half the strands of one group with half the strands of the adjacent group 1" (2.5 cm) down from the first knot. Trim ends to even lengths. Note: Sample shows bobble rope (page 150) sewn above fringe.

Triple Knot Fringe with Welt

To make a welt, work 2 rows St st, mark this row with fine cotton thread, work 6 more rows St st. Slip sts of marked row onto fine dpn. Place dpn behind and parallel to sts on working needle. **Welt:** *K2tog (1 st from front needle with 1 st from dpn); rep from *. Cont in desired patt. Work double knot fringe (above) across edge of work. Then tie a third row of knots 1" (2.5 cm) below the previous row of knots, again working together half the strands of one group with half the strands of the adjacent group. Embroider cross st (page 190) on top of welt, if desired.

Friseur Fringe

CO 23 sts.
Rows 1, 2, 5, and 6: Knit.
Rows 3 and 7: BO 19 sts, knit to end—4 sts.
Row 4: K4, cable CO 19 sts (page 259).
Rep Rows 4–7 for desired length, BO all sts on Row 7.

Loop-d-Lou

(multiple of 2 sts + 1)

Form the loops as you work the background. Apply a Single Knot Fringe to each loop section later.

Rows 1–6: Knit.

Row 7: *K1, [yo] 4 times; rep from *.

Row 8: Knit, dropping 3 extra loops from each yo.

Rep Rows 3–8 for each row of fringe. BO all sts.

Fringe: Cut groups of lengths of yarn twice the desired length, plus 1" (2.5 cm) extra for knotting. *Fold each group in half to form a loop, and with RS of work facing, insert crochet hook through a group of 4 long sts, from back to front, draw the loop through, then draw yarn ends through loop and tighten; rep from *.

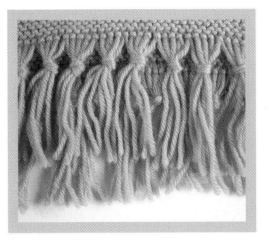

Corkscrew Fringe

The fringes are knitted separately and then attached. The length of fringe will depend on yarn weight and number of stitches cast on.

CO desired number of sts.

Row 1: (K1f&b, k1) in each st.

Row 2: BO all sts pwise.

Use your fingers to twist each tassel into a corkscrew.

Garter-Stitch Fringe

CO 16 sts. Work garter st for desired length. BO 8 sts. Break yarn and draw tail through rem st on right needle. Sl rem sts off left needle and unravel them every row. Working from right to left, knot loops of 6 adjacent rows.

Seed-Stitch Fringe

CO 17 sts.

Row 1: *K1, p1; rep from *, end k1.

Rep Row 1 for desired length. BO 9 sts. Cut yarn and pull tail through rem st on right needle. Sl rem sts off left needle and unravel them every row. Cut rem loops and knot into groups.

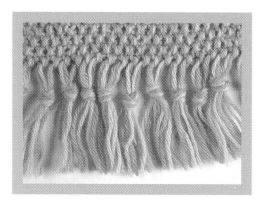

Contrast Cable Fringe

With A, CO 9 sts, and then with B, CO 5 sts—14 sts total.

Rows 1 and 5: (RS) With B, k5, with A, k9.

Rows 2, 4, 6, and 8: Purl with established colors.

Row 3: With B, k5, with A, 3/3LC, k3.

Row 7: With B, k5, with A, k3, 3/3RC.

Rep Rows 1–8 for desired length, end with a RS row. With WS facing, BO 10 sts, cut yarn, and pull tail through rem st on right needle. Sl rem sts off left needle and unravel them every row. Cut loops.

Pillow trimmed with cable fringe.

Plaited Fringe

CO 18 sts.

Rows 1 and 3: (WS) K2, p8, k2, p6.

Row 2: K6, p2, [2/2RC] 2 times, p2.

Row 4: K6, p2, k2, 2/2LC, k2, p2.

Rep Rows 1–4 for desired length, end with a RS row. With WS facing, BO 13 sts, cut yarn, and pull tail through rem st on right needle. Sl rem sts off left needle and unravel them every row.

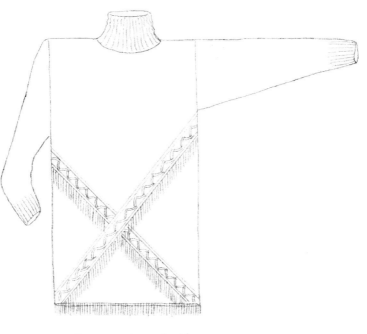

Sweater trimmed with plaited fringe.

Split Cable Fringe

With A, CO 21 sts.

Row 1: (RS) With A, k12, with B, p1, k1, p1, with A, k6.

Rows 2 and 4: With A, p6, with B, p1, k1, p1, with A, p12.

Row 3: With A, K6, 2/2RC, with B, p1, k1, p1, with A, 2/2LC.

Rep Rows 1–4 for desired length. With WS facing, BO 15 sts, cut yarn, and pull tail through rem st on right needle. Sl rem sts off left needle and unravel them every row.

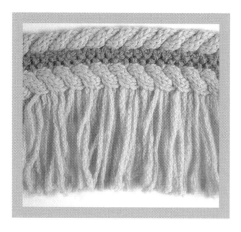

Celtic Princess Braid Fringe

CO 34 sts.

Set-up row: (WS) P1, k3, [p6, k4] 2 times, p3, k1, p6.

Row 1: (RS) K6, p1, k3, [p4, 3/3LC] 2 times, p3, k1.

Rows 2, 4, 6, and 8: Knit the knits and purl the purls.

Row 3: K6, p1, [3/2LCP, 3/2RCP] 2 times, 3/2LCP, p1, k1.

Row 5: K6, p3, [3/3RC, p4] 2 times, k3, p1, k1.

Row 7: K6, p1, [3/2RCP, 3/2LCP] 2 times, 3/2 RCP, p1, k1.

Rep Rows 1–8 for desired length, end with a RS row. With WS facing, BO 28 sts, cut yarn, and pull tail through rem st on right needle. Sl rem sts off left needle and unravel them every row. Cut fringe loops. Sew pearl bead in center of each "p4" segment.

Woven Braid Fringe

CO 22 sts.

Rows 1 and 5: Knit.

Rows 2, 4, 6, and 8: Purl.

Row 3: K7, [3/3LC] 2 times, k3.

Row 7: K4, [3/3RC] 3 times.

Rep Rows 1–8 for desired length, end with a RS row. With WS facing, BO 18 sts, cut yarn, and pull tail through rem st on right needle. Sl rem sts off left needle and unravel them every row.

Imperial Bead Fringe

Notes: See pages 262–263 for instructions on knitting with beads. String 17 beads onto knitting yarn for each patt rep. Slip all sts kwise.

SB1: Slip 1 bead as close as possible to left needle. CO 12 sts.

Row 1: Sl 1, k11, turn.

Row 2: SB1, k7, yo, k1, [yo, k2tog] 2 times—13 sts.

Row 3: Sl 1, k3, p1, k8.

Row 4: SB1, k7, yo, k2, [yo, k2tog] 2 times—14 sts.

Row 5: Sl 1, k3, p2, k8.

Row 6: SB1, k7, yo, k3, [yo, k2tog] 2 times—15 sts.

Row 7: Sl 1, k3, p3, k8.

Row 8: SB1, k7, yo, k4, [yo, k2tog] 2 times—16 sts.

Row 9: Sl 1, k3, p4, k8.

Row 10: SB1, k7, yo, k5, [yo, k2tog] 2 times—17 sts.

Row 11: Sl 1, k3, p5, k8.

Row 12: SB1, k7, yo, k6, [yo, k2tog] 2 times—18 sts.

Row 13: Sl 1, k3, p6, k8.

Row 14: SB1, k7, yo, k7, [yo, k2tog] 2 times—19 sts.

Row 15: Sl 1, k3, p7, k8.

Row 16: SB1, k7, yo, k8, [yo, k2tog] 2 times—20 sts.

Row 17: Sl 1, k3, p8, k8.

Row 18: SB1, k7, yo, k2tog, k7, [yo, k2tog] 2 times—19 sts.

Row 19: Sl 1, k3, p6, p2tog, k8.

Row 20: SB1, k7, yo, k2tog, k6, [yo, k2tog] 2 times.

Row 21: Sl 1, k3, p5, p2tog, k8—18 sts.

Row 22: SB1, k7, yo, k2tog, k5, [yo, k2tog] 2 times.

Row 23: Sl 1, k3, p4, p2tog, k8—17 sts.

Row 24: SB1, k7, yo, k2tog, k4, [yo, k2tog] 2 times.

Row 25: Sl 1, k3, p3, p2tog, k8—16 sts.

Row 26: SB1, k7, yo, k2tog, k3, [yo, k2tog] 2 times.

Row 27: Sl 1, k3, p2, p2tog, k8—15 sts.

Lamp shade with imperial bead fringe.

217

Row 28: SB1, k7, yo, k2tog, k2, [yo, k2tog] 2 times.

Row 29: Sl 1, k3, p1, p2tog, k8—14 sts.

Row 30: SB1, k7, k2tog, k1, [yo, k2tog] 2 times—13 sts.

Row 31: Sl 1, k3, p2tog, k7—12 sts.

Row 32: SB1, k7, k1, [yo, k2tog] 2 times.

Rep rows 1–32 for desired length, end with a RS row. With WS facing, BO 6 sts, cut yarn, and pull tail through rem st on right needle. Sl rem sts off left needle and unravel them every row. Knot fringe above each bead. Sew additional beads to St st areas.

Feather Knot Fringe

Note: On RS, knit through the back loop of all but the first 5 sts. On WS, purl all purl sts through the back loop; knit all knit sts as usual. Work all cables in reverse on WS; the direction that the sts move in is constant.

CO 20 sts.

Foundation row: (WS) K1, p1b, k5, [p1b] 2 times, k5, p1b, k5.

Rows 1, 3 and 5: K5, k1b, p5, 1/1LC, p5, k1b, p1.

Rows 2, 4, and 6: K1, p1b, k5, [p1b] 2 times, k5, p1b, k5.

Row 7: K5, k1b, p4, 1/1RCP, 1/1LCP, p4, k1b, p1.

Row 8: K1, p1b, k3, 1/1LC, k2, 1/1RC, k3, p1b, k5.

Row 9: K5, k1b, p2, 1/1RCP, k1b, p2, k1b, 1/1LCP, p2, k1b, p1.

Row 10: K1, p1b, k1, 1/1LC, k1, p1b, k2, p1b, k1, 1/1RC, k1, p1b, k5.

Row 11: K5, k1b, 1/1RCP, k1b, p1, 1/1LC, 1/1RC, p1, k1b, 1/1LCP, k1b, p1.

Row 12: K1, ([p1b] 2 times, k1) 4 times, [p1b] 2 times, k5.

Row 13: K5, [k1b] 2 times, p1, 1/1RCP, p2, [k1b] 2 times, p2, 1/1LCP, p1, [k1b] 2 times, p1.

Row 14: K1, [p1b] 2 times, 1/1LCP, k1, 1/1LC, 1/1RC, k1, 1/1RCP, [p1b] 2 times, k5.

Row 15: K5, [k1b] 2 times, p2, 1/1RCP, [k1b] 2 times, 1/1LCP, p2, [k1b] 2 times, p1.

Row 16: K1, p1b, k2, 1/1LCP, k1, [p1b] 2 times, k1, 1/1RCP, k2, p1b, k5.

Rows 17 and 23: K5, k1b, p4, 1/1RC, 1/1LC, p4, k1b, p1.

Rows 18 and 24: K1, p1b, k3, p1b, k1, [p1b] 2 times, k1, p1b, k3, p1b, k5.

Rows 19 and 25: K5, [k1b, p2] 2 times, [k1b] 2 times, [p2, k1b] 2 times, p1.

Rows 20 and 26: K1, p1b, k4, 1/1LC, 1/1RC, k4, p1b, k5.

Rows 21 and 27: K5, k1b, p3, 1/1RCP, [k1b] 2 times, 1/1LCP, p3, k1b, p1.

Rows 22 and 28: K1, [p1b, k2] 2 times, [p1b] 2 times, [k2, p1b] 2 times, k5.

Row 29: K5, k1b, p4, 1/1RCP, 1/1LCP, p4, k1b, p1.

Row 30: K1, p1b, k4, p1b, k2, p1b, k4, p1b, k5.

Row 31: K5, k1b, p4, 1/1LCP, 1/1RCP, p4, k1b, p1.

Row 32: K1, p1b, k5, [p1b] 2 times, k5, p1b, k5.

Rows 33 and 35: Rep Row 1.

Rows 34 and 36: Rep Row 2.

Rep Rows 1–36 for desired length. Slip a bugle bead onto each loop.

Autumnal Leaf

CO 13 sts.

Foundation row: (WS) [K5, p1] 2 times, k1.

Row 1: (RS) P1, k1b, p2, ([k1, k1b, yo] 2 times, k1, k1b) in
same st, p2, k1b, k5—20 sts.

Row 2: K5, p1b, k2, p8, k2, p1b, k1.

Row 3: P1, k1b, p2, k6, k2tog, p2, k1b, k5—19 sts.

Row 4: K5, p1b, k2, p7, k2, p1b, k1.

Row 5: P1, k1b, p2, k5, k2tog, p2, k1b, k5—18 sts.

Row 6: K5, p1b, k2, p6, k2, p1b, k1.

Row 7: P1, k1b, p2, k4, k2tog, p2, k1b, k5—17 sts.

Row 8: K5, p1b, k2, p5, k2, p1b, k1.

Row 9: P1, k1b, p2, k3, k2tog, p2, k1b, k5—16 sts.

Row 10: K5, p1b, k2, p4, k2, p1b, k1.

Row 11: P1, k1b, p2, k2, k2tog, p2, k1b, k5—15 sts.

Row 12: K5, p1b, k2, p3, k2, p1b, k1.

Row 13: P1, k1b, p2, k1, k2tog, p2, k1b, k5—14 sts.

Row 14: K5, p1b, k2, p2, k2, p1b, k1.

Row 15: P1, k1b, p2, k2tog, p2, k1b, k5—13 sts.

Row 16: K5, p1b, k2, p1, k2, p1b, k1.

Rep Rows 1–16 for desired length, end with a WS row. With RS facing, BO 8 sts, cut yarn, and pull tail
through rem st on right needle. Sl rem sts off left needle and unravel them every row.

For twisted fringe, place a long tapestry needle at base of fringe loop, twist the needle clockwise until
the loop kinks, then steam lightly. (Note: This works best with wool yarn.)

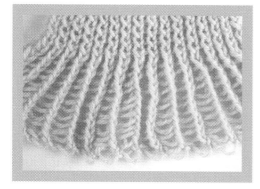

Gossamer Fringe

(multiple of 3 sts + 1)

Rows 1, 3, 5, 7, 9, and 11: K1b, *p2, k1b; rep from *.

Rows 2, 4, 6, 8, 10, and 12: P1, *k1b, k1, p1; rep from *.

Row 13: K1b, *sl next st off needle and allow it to unravel to CO edge, p1, k1b; rep from *—mult of 2 sts + 1.

Rows 14, 16, and 18: P1, *k1b, p1; rep from *.

Rows 15, 17, and 19: K1b, *p1, k1b; rep from *.

Loop Stitch

(multiple of 2 sts + 1)

This pattern is worked on a St st base. Yarn is wrapped around the left thumb to form loops.

Row 1: (RS) K1, *(k1 and leave st on left needle, yf, wrap yarn clockwise once around left thumb to make loop, yb, knit into back of same st), k1; rep from *.

Row 2: P1, *p2tog, p1; rep from *.

Row 3: K2, *make loop as before, k1; rep from *, end last rep k2.

Row 4: P2, *p2tog, p1; rep from *, end last rep p2.

Rep Rows 1–4 for desired length.

Faux Fur

(multiple of 2 sts + 1)

The loops in this stitch are formed on the front of the work but are worked from the wrong side. Form the loop by wrapping the yarn around one or more fingers, depending on the length of loops desired. The loops can later be cut or left uncut.

Make loop: Insert needle in st, wrap yarn over needle kwise, then wrap yarn over 1 or 2 fingers of left hand, then over needle again, draw both loops on needle through the st and place them on left needle, knit the 2 loops tog tbl (drawing on page 62).

Rows 1 and 3: (RS) Knit.

Row 2: K1, *make loop, k1; rep from *.

Row 4: K2, *make loop, k1; rep from *, end last rep k2.

Rep Rows 1–4 for desired length.

Tassels

Tassels may be used for many decorative purposes—to embellish garments, to top a hat, or as borders. They may also be used on home decorations such as curtain tiebacks, pillows, and afghans. The following instructions are for wrapped, knitted, and beaded tassels. Use any type of yarn or yarn combination. The loops at the base may be cut or left uncut, as desired.

Basic Tassel

Cut a piece of cardboard 4" (10 cm) wide by the desired length of the tassel plus 1" (2.5 cm) for tying and trimming. Wrap yarn 40 times (or to desired thickness) around length of cardboard. Cut a piece of yarn about 18" (46 cm) long and thread doubled onto a tapestry needle. Insert needle under all strands at upper edge of cardboard. Pull tightly and knot securely near strands. Unless you want loops at the base of the tassel (bottom photo), cut yarn loops at lower edge of cardboard. Cut a piece of yarn 12" (30.5 cm) long and wrap tightly around loops 1½" (3.8 cm) below top knot to form tassel neck. Knot securely, thread ends onto tapestry needle and pull ends to center of tassel. Trim tassel ends evenly.

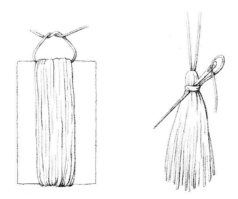

Tassels Combined with Fringe

Make single knot fringe (page 211) and basic tassel (page 221). Sample shows a repeat of 3 fringes and 1 tassel attached to a seed-stitch background. Any combination of fringe and tassels may be used on any type background.

Scarf edged with tassels and fringe.

One-Ball Tassel with Knitted Band

Make basic tassel but do not tie neck. Insert 1" (2.5-cm) Styrofoam ball and tie neck below ball. To make band, CO number of sts needed to fit around neck with needles corresponding to yarn weight. Knit 2 rows. BO all sts. Wrap band close to base of ball. Sew CO edge to BO edge. Work the band with CC for a different look.

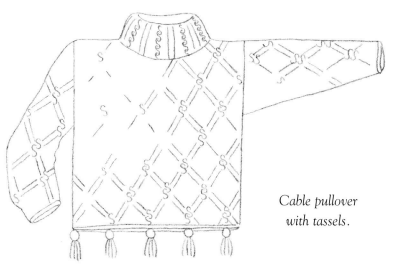

Cable pullover with tassels.

222

Two-Ball Tassel with Knitted Tie

Make as One-Ball Tassel (page 222), but wrap tassel around a longer piece of cardboard to allow for second ball. Insert and tie second ball below first. Make 2 bands as for One-Ball Tassel and wrap 1 band close to the base of each ball.

Tassel Border

Make a length of twisted cord (page 266) and mark every 2¼" (5.5 cm) with pins. Make desired number of Basic Tassels (page 221). *Tie tassels to twisted cord at center between pins; rep from *. Beg at left side, sew to knitted back at each pin marker. Remove pins.

Finial Tassel

With CC, CO 12 sts. Change to MC.

Row 1: (RS) *K1, M1; rep from *, end k1—23 sts.

Row 2: P1, *k1, p1; rep from *.

Cont in 1x1 rib as established for 1½" (3.8 cm), end with a
  WS row.

Row 3: K1, *k2tog; rep from *—12 sts.

Row 4: K1f&b, *k1, p1; rep from *—13 sts.

Row 5: *K1, p1, M1 pwise; rep from *, end k1—19 sts

Row 6: *P1, k2; rep from *, end p1.

Row 7: *K1, p2, M1 pwise; rep from *, end p1—25 sts.

Row 8: *P1, k3; rep from *, end p1.

Row 9: *K1, p3, M1 pwise; rep from *, end pl—31 sts.

Cont working M1 pwise incs every RS row in this manner, working one more purl st bet incs, and working established rib on WS rows until there are 49 sts. Change to CC. Knit 2 rows. BO all sts. Insert 1" (2.5-cm) Styrofoam ball into top of tassel and sew seam. Wrap yarn around tassel near base of ball. Make tie and secure close to base of ball. Sew beads around neck and 1 bead at each knit stitch point on BO edge.

*Pullover with
V-cables and
tassels.*

Baby Cable Tassel

With CC, CO 30 sts. Change to MC.

Rows 1 and 3: (WS) K2, *p2, k2; rep from *.

Row 2: P2, *k2, p2; rep from *.

Row 4: P2, *k2tog and leave sts on needle, knit first st again, slip both sts off needle, p2; rep from *.

Rep Rows 1–4 for 2" (5 cm) or desired length of skirt, end with Row 3.

Next row: P2, *k2tog, p2; rep from *—23 sts.

Change to CC. Purl 2 rows. Cont in rev St st for 1½" (3.8 cm), end with a RS row.

Next row: (WS) K1, *k2tog; rep from *—12 sts.

Next row: *P2tog; rep from *—6 sts. Cut yarn, leaving a long tail. Thread tail on tapestry needle, and pull through rem sts on needle. Gather up and fasten securely. Make twisted cord (page 266) and attach to top.

Two-Color Cable Tassel

This tassel looks best when worked in worsted weight yarn. If you use lighter weight yarn, add more pattern repeats.

With A, CO 17 sts. Join B and work Two-Color Mock Cable Rib (page 100) for 14 rows. Cont with A only, working dec rows as follows:

Row 1: (WS) *P2tog, p3; rep from *, end p2tog—13 sts.

Rows 2–6: Beg with a knit row, work in St st.

Row 7: P1, *p2tog; rep from *—7 sts.

Row 8: K1, *k2tog; rep from *—4 sts.

Cut yarn, leaving a long tail. Thread tail on tapestry needle, and pull through rem sts on needle. Gather up and fasten securely. Insert 1" (2.5-cm) Styrofoam ball into top of tassel and sew seam. Wrap yarn around tassel near base of ball.

Scalloped Tassel

Cast on 57 sts.

Work Rows 1–3 of Scalloped Edging with Rib (page 131)—32 sts.

Knit 1 row. Work 1x1 rib for 2" (5 cm). *Next row:* K1, *k2tog, k1; rep from * to last st, k1—22 sts. Cont in St st for 1" (2.5 cm), ending with a WS row. *Next row:* (RS): *K2tog; rep from *—11 sts. *Next row:* P1, *p2tog; rep from *—6 sts. Cut yarn, leaving a long tail. Thread tail on tapestry needle, pull through rem sts. Gather up and fasten securely. With CC, work French knots (page 203) on top. Sew seam. Insert 1" (2.5-cm) Styrofoam ball into top of tassel and tie at neck. With CC, make a twisted cord (page 266) and wrap around tassel close to base of ball. Sew roses to bottom edge.

French Lace Tassel

CO 28 sts.

Rows 1, 2, 3, 5, 7, 9, and 11: Purl.

Row 4, 6, 8, and 10: K1, *k2tog, k2, yo, k1, yo, k2, k2tog; rep from *.

Row 12: K1, *k2tog, k1; rep from *—19 sts.

Rows 13–18: Knit.

Row 19: K1, *k2tog; rep from *—10 sts.

Cut yarn leaving a long tail. Thread tail on tapestry needle and pull through rem sts on needle. Gather up and fasten securely. Insert 1" (2.5-cm) Styrofoam ball into top of tassel or stuff with fiberfill. Sew seam. Wrap yarn around bottom of ball for neck.

Cord Fleur Tassel

Knit cord (page 149) is used to form the flowers at base of attached cord. It may be used alone or in groups. To form the flowers, draw the end of the cord into the desired number of loops and sew in place.

Corkscrew Tassel Trio

Make 3 corkscrew fringes (page 213), each a different length. Sew the 3 cords tog at one end.

Beaded Tassel I

In this tassel, size 11° seed beads, large faceted, and small faceted beads are sewn in place after the piece is knitted. The sample is worked in fine novelty yarn on size 000 (1.5 mm) needles.

Ball: CO 6 sts.

Row 1: (RS) Knit.

Row 2: P1, *p1f&b; rep from * to last st, p1—10 sts.

Row 3: K1, *k1f&b; rep from * to last st, k1—18 sts.

Row 4: Purl.

Row 5: *K2 [k1f&b] 5 times, k2; rep from *—28 sts.

Rows 6–10, 13–16, and 19–20: Work in St st.

Rows 11–12, 17–18, and 21–22: With CC, knit.

Row 23: K1, *k2tog; rep from *, end k1—15 sts.

Row 24: P1, *p2tog; rep from *—8 sts.

Cut yarn, leaving a long tail. Thread tail on a tapestry needle, pull through rem sts. Gather up and fasten securely. Insert 1" (2.5-cm) Styrofoam ball into top of tassel and sew seam. String beads on thread for desired length and sew to top of ball for hanging. Sew alternating small and large faceted beads between the 1st and 2nd garter ridges and small faceted beads between the 2nd and 3rd garter ridges. **Streamers:** (Make 11) String beads and attach to bottom of ball. With CC, CO 8 sts. On next row, BO all sts. Sew around bottom of ball above streamers.

Beaded Tassel II

This tassel is worked in bead knitting with #5 embroidery cotton on size 000 (1.5 mm) needles. See pages 262–263 for instructions on knitting with beads.

Beads: 1 vial hex-cut beads; 15 #5 bugle beads; 30 #3 bugle beads; 45 small faceted beads.

Thread hex-cut beads onto knitting yarn.

Ball: Using the provisional method, CO 35 sts. Maintaining an edge st on each end, work in bead knitting for 2". K1, *k3tog; rep from *, end k1—13 sts. P1, *p2tog; rep from *—7 sts. Cut yarn, leaving a long tail. Thread tail on a tapestry needle and pull through rem sts. Fasten off. Place provisional sts on needle. With RS facing, k1, *k3tog; rep from *, end k1—13 sts. P1, *p2tog; rep from *—7 sts. Cut yarn, and draw tail through rem sts. Gather up and fasten securely. Insert 1½" (3.8-cm) Styrofoam ball into top of tassel and sew seam. String hex-beads on thread for desired length of hanging loop. Sew to top of ball.

Streamers: (make 15) Using beading needle and waxed thread, string one #5 bugle bead, *3 hex-beads, 1 faceted bead, 3 hex-beads, one #3 bugle bead; rep from * once, 3 hex-beads, 1 faceted bead, end 1 bugle bead. Pass beading needle and waxed thread from bottom to top through all beads beginning with lowest faceted bead. Leave long ends to sew to bottom of ball. Stitch all streamers to bottom of ball.

Looped skirt: Sew end of new waxed thread to bottom of ball outside the stitched streamers. *String 25 hex-beads and stitch to bottom of ball; rep from * 10 more times.

Beaded Tassel III

This tassel is worked in the bead knitting technique with #5 embroidery cotton on size 000 (1.5 mm) needles. See pages 262–263 for instructions on knitting with beads.

Beads: 1 vial hex-cut beads; 39 #2 bugle beads; 26 medium faceted beads; 13 flower beads; 13 teardrop beads.

Thread hex-cut beads onto knitting yarn.

Ball: Work as for Beaded Tassel II (page 228).

Streamers: (make 13) Using beading needle and waxed thread string 1 bugle bead, *3 hex-beads, 1 faceted bead, 3 hex-beads, 1 bugle bead; rep from * once, 1 flower, end 1 teardrop bead. Pass beading needle and waxed thread from bottom to top through all beads beginning with flower bead. Leave long ends to sew to bottom of ball. Stitch all streamers to bottom of ball.

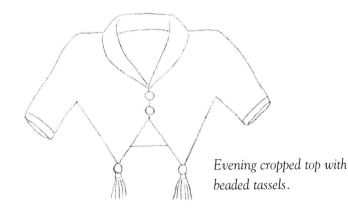

Evening cropped top with beaded tassels.

Beaded Tassel IV

This tassel is worked in the beaded knitting technique with #5 embroidery cotton on size 000 (1.5 mm) needles. See pages 262–263 for instructions on knitting with beads.

Beads: 1 vial size 11° seed beads; 42 11 seed beads in CC; 30 #2 bugle beads; 12 medium faceted beads; 14 small faceted beads in CC.

Thread seed beads onto knitting yarn.

Ball: Using the provisional method, CO 34 sts.

Rows 1, 3 and 5: (RS) K2 *SB1, k1b; rep from *, end last rep k2.

Rows 2 and 4: P2, *SB1, p1b; rep from *

Rows 6–8: Work in St st without any beads.

Row 9: K2, *SB15, k1b, k2; rep from *, end last rep k1.

Rows 10, 12, 14, 16, 18, and 20: Purl.

Row 11: K1, *SB11, k1b, k2; rep from *.

Row 13: K2, *SB11, k1b, k2; rep from *, end last rep k1.

Row 15: K1, *SB11, k1b, k2; rep from *.

Row 17: K2, *SB11, k1b, k2; rep from *, end last rep k1.

Row 19: K1, *SB11, k1b, k2; rep from *.

Row 21: K1, *k2tog; rep from *, end k1—18 sts.

Row 22: P1, *p2tog; rep from *, end p1—10 sts.

Cut yarn, leaving a long tail. Thread tail on a tapestry needle and pull through rem sts. Gather up and fasten securely. Insert 1" (2.5-cm) Styrofoam ball into top of tassel and sew seam. String beads on waxed thread for desired length of hanging loop. Sew to top of ball.

Streamers: (Make 9) Using beading needle and waxed thread string *5 seed beads, 1 bugle bead, 5 seed beads, 1 CC seed bead, 1 faceted bead, 1 CC seed bead; rep from * once, 1 medium faceted bead, 1 seed bead. Pass beading needle and waxed thread from bottom to top through all beads beginning with medium faceted bead. Leave long ends to sew to bottom of ball. Stitch all streamers to bottom of ball.

Beaded Tassel V

This tassel is worked in the beaded knitting technique with #5 embroidery cotton on size 000 (1.5 mm) needles. See pages 262–263 for instructions on knitting with beads.

Beads: 1 vial size 11° seed beads; 121 size 11° seed beads in CC; 84 #2 bugle beads; 12 large teardrop beads; 36 small teardrop beads in CC.

Thread seed beads onto knitting yarn.

SB1: Slide specified number of beads (in this case, 1) close to right needle.

Ball: CO 6 sts. Note: Maintain an edge st on each end of needle.

Row 1: (RS) Knit.

Row 2: K1, *k1f&b; rep from * to last st, k1—10 sts.

Row 3: K2, *SB1, k1b; rep from * end last rep k2.

Row 4: K1, *k1f&b; rep from * to last st, k1—18 sts.

Row 5: K2, *SB1, k1b; rep from *, end last rep k2.

Row 6: K1, *k1f&b; rep from * to last st, k1—34 sts.

Rows 7 and 21: K2, *SB21, k1b, k1; rep from *.

Rows 8–10: Knit.

Rows 11 and 19: K1, *SB23, k1b, k1; rep from *, end last rep k2.

Rows 12–14. Knit.

Row 15: K2, *SB23, k1b, k1; rep from *.

Rows 16–18: Knit.

Rows 20, 22, and 24: Knit.

Row 23: K1, *SB21, k1b, k1; rep from *, end last rep k2.

Row 25: K2, *SB17, k3; rep from *.

Row 26: K1, [k2tog] 16 times, k1—18 sts.

Row 27: K1, *SB11, k1b, k1; rep from *, end last rep k2.

Row 28: K1, [k2tog] 8 times, k1—10 sts.

Row 29: K2, *SB11, k1b, k1; rep from *.

Row 30: K1, [k2tog] 4 times, k1—6 sts.

Row 31: K1, *SB1, k1b; rep from *, end last rep k2.

Cut yarn, leaving a long tail. Thread tail on a tapestry needle and pull through rem sts. Gather up and fasten securely. Insert 1" (2.5-cm) Styrofoam ball into top of tassel and sew seam. String seed and bugle beads on waxed thread for desired length of hanging loop. Sew to top of ball.

Streamers: (Make 12) Using beading needle and waxed thread, string 11 seed beads, [1 CC seed bead, 1 bugle bead] twice, 1 CC seed bead, 9 seed beads, 1 CC seed bead, 1 bugle bead, 1 CC seed bead,

3 seed beads, 1 CC seed bead, 1 bugle bead, 1 CC seed bead, 5 seed beads, 1 large teardrop bead, 3 small teardrop beads. Pass beading needle and waxed thread from bottom to top beginning with large teardrop bead, then 5 seed beads. Separately, string 1 CC seed bead, 1 bugle bead, 1 CC seed bead, 3 seed beads, 1 CC seed bead, 1 bugle bead, 1 CC seed bead, then pass needle through all rem beads. Stitch all streamers to bottom of ball.

Reverse Stockinette-Stitch Beaded Tassel

This tassel is worked in the beaded knitting technique with #5 embroidery cotton on size 000 (1.5 mm) needles. See pages 262–263 for instructions on knitting with beads.

Beads: 1 vial faceted beads; 48 hex-beads; 10 bell-shaped beads; 11 heart-shaped beads; 33 flat circular beads.

Rev St st is right side of tassel.

Thread faceted beads onto knitting yarn. *Note:* Maintain an edge st at each end of needle.

Ball: CO 6 sts.

Row 1: (RS) Purl.

Row 2: K1, *k1f&b; rep from * to last st, k1—10 sts.

Row 3: P1, *p1f&b; rep from * to last st, p1—18 sts.

Row 4: K1, *k1f&b; rep from * to last st, k1—34 sts.

Row 5: P2, *SB1, p3; rep from * end last rep p2.

Rows 6–8: Work Rev St st.

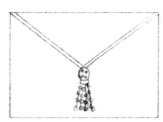

Envelope bag with beaded tassel.

Rows 9–20: Rep rows 5—8 three times.

Row 21: P1, [p2tog] 16 times, p1—18 sts.

Row 22: K1, [k2tog] 8 times, k1—10 sts.

Cut yarn, leaving a long tail. Thread tail on a tapestry needle and pull through rem sts. Gather up and fasten securely. Insert 1½" (3.8-cm) Styrofoam ball into top of tassel and sew seam. String seed and bugle beads on waxed thread for desired length hanging loop. Sew to top of ball.

Streamers: (Make 9) Using beading needle and waxed thread, string 1 faceted bead [3 hex-beads, 1 flat circular] 3 times, 3 hex-beads, 3 faceted beads, 3 hex-beads, 1 heart-shaped bead, 1 hex-cut bead, 1 bell-shaped bead, 1 faceted bead. Beg with bell-shaped bead, insert needle back through all beads. Attach streamers to bottom of ball.

Garter-Stitch Tassel

Note: Sample worked with 1 strand each of 2 yarns.

CO 22 sts. Work Garter Stitch Fringe (page 213) for 3½" (9 cm). BO 12 sts, cut yarn, and pull tail through rem st on right needle. Sl rem sts off left needle and unravel them every row.

Thread tail on tapestry needle and beg 2 sts from top edge, weave yarn in and out of every other st. Leave ends free. Insert 1" (2.5-cm) Styrofoam ball into top of tassel and sew seam. Make twisted cord (page 266) and secure to top of tassel. Tie at neck one row above unraveled portion. Tie tightly and wrap yarn around neck.

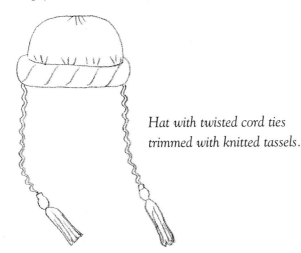

Hat with twisted cord ties trimmed with knitted tassels.

Gossamer Tassel

CO 37 sts. Rep Rows 1 and 2 of Gossamer Fringe (page 220) for 3" (7.5 cm), ending with a WS row. *Next row:* K1b, *sl next st off needle and allow it to drop to CO edge, p1, k1b; rep from *—25 sts.

Row 1: P1, *k1b, p1; rep from *.

Row 2: K1b, *p1, k1b; rep from *.

Rep Rows 1 and 2 for a total of 12 rows.

Cut yarn leaving a long tail. Thread tail on tapestry needle and pull through rem sts on needle. Gather up and fasten securely. Insert 1" (2.5-cm) Styrofoam ball into top of tassel or stuff with fiberfill. Sew seam. Wrap yarn around base of ball. Make tie and secure to top. Thread tapestry needle with ¼" (6 mm) satin ribbon, and beg at center front, weave in and out of every other stitch. Tie ribbon into bow.

Romeo's Tassel Border

(multiple of 11 sts + 2)

Make Tassel: Insert needle into st kwise, [wind yarn clockwise around 2 fingers and needle] 5 times, draw all 5 loops through the stitch and place them on the left needle, then knit them tog through back loops (see page 27).

CO 57 sts.

Row 1: (RS) Purl.

Row 2: K6, *make tassel, k10; rep from *, end last rep k6.

Row 3: P6, *k1f&b of 5-st group of previous row, p10; rep from *, end last rep p6—mult of 12 sts + 2.

Row 4: K6, *p2, k10; rep from *, end last rep k6.

Row 5: P5, *1/1RCP, 11LCP, p8; rep from *, end last rep p5.

Row 6 and even-numbered rows through 26: Knit the knits and purl the purls.

Row 7: P4, *1/1RCP, p2, 1/1LCP, p6; rep from *, end last rep p4.

Row 9: P3, *1/1RCP, p4, 1/1LCP, p4; rep from *, end last rep p3.

Row 11: P2, *1/1RCP, p6, 1/1LCP, p2; rep from *, end last rep p2.

Row 13: P1, *1/1RCP, p8, 1/1LCP; rep from *, end last rep p1.

Row 15: P1, k1, *p10, 1/1LC; rep from *, end p10, k1, p1.

Row 17: P1, *1/1LCP, p8, 1/1RCP; rep from *, end last rep p1.

Row 19: P2, *1/1LCP, p6, 1/1RCP, p2; rep from *, end last rep p2.

Row 21: P3, *1/1LCP, p4, 1/1RCP, p4; rep from *, end last rep p3.

Row 23: P4, *1/1LCP, p2, 1/1RCP, p6; rep from *, end last rep p4.

Row 25: P5, *1/1LCP, 1/1RCP, p8; rep from *, end last rep p5.

Row 27: P6, *k2tog, p10; rep from *, end last rep p6.

Rows 28–34: Work even in rev St st.

BO all sts.

Cut and trim tassels. Sew rhinestones in center of diamonds, if desired.

Juliet's Tassel Border

(multiple of 11 sts + 1)

Make Tassel: Insert needle into st kwise, [wind yarn clockwise around 2 fingers and needle] 5 times, draw all 5 loops through the stitch and place them on the left needle, then knit them tog through back loops.

CO 56 sts.

Row 1: (RS) Purl.

Row 2: K5, *p2, k4, make tassel, k4; rep from *, end last rep p2, k5.

Row 3: P5, *1/1RC, p4, k5tog, knit in back of same st, p4; rep from *, end last rep 1/1RC, p5.

Row 4 and all even-numbered rows through 14: Knit the knits and purl the purls.

Row 5: P4, *1/1RC, 1/1LC, p8; rep from *, end last rep p4.

Row 7: P3, *1/1RC, k2, 1/1LC, p6; rep from *, end last rep p3.

Row 9: P2, *1/1RC, k4, 1/1LC, p4; rep from *, end last rep p2.

Row 11: P1, *1/1RC, k6, 1/1LC, p2; rep from *, end last rep p1.

Row 13: *1/1RC, k8, 1/1LC; rep from *, end last rep 1/1LC.

Row 15: *K10, 1/1RC; rep from *, end last rep k10.

Rows 16–24: Work even in St st.

BO all sts.

Cut and trim tassels. Sew rhinestones at top of purl points, if desired. Embroider straight sts (page 192) and daisy sts (page 202) in each triangular section.

Petruchio Tassel Border

(multiple of 12 sts + 1)

Make Tassel: Insert needle into st kwise and at needle point, [wind yarn around 4 fingers and needle] 5 times, draw all 5 loops through the stitch and place them on the left needle, then knit them tog through back loops.

With A, CO 61 sts.

Row 1: (RS) Seed 61 sts.

Row 2: With A, seed 6, with B, make tassel, with A, seed 11; rep from *, end last rep seed 6 with A.

Row 3: With A, seed 6, *with B, k1, with A, seed 11; rep from *, end last seed 6 with A.

Row 4: With A, seed 5, *with B, p3, with A, seed 9; rep from *, end last rep seed 5 with A.

Row 5: With A, seed 4, *with B, k5, with A, seed 7; rep from *, end last rep seed 4 with A.

Row 6: With A, seed 3, *with B, p7, with A, seed 5; rep from *, end last rep seed 3 with A.

Row 7: With A, seed 2, *with B, k9, with A, seed 3; rep from *, end last rep seed 2 with A.

Row 8: With A, seed 1, *with B, p11, with A, seed 1; rep from *.

Row 9: *With A, k1, with B, k11; rep from *, end k1 with A.

Cont in St st in established colors for desired length. Sew rhinestones at top of tassels if desired.

Pom-Poms

Pom-poms are often underrated. They may be used for much more than adorning the top of a hat.

Many gadgets on the market aid in making fringes, tassels, pom-poms and ties. These gadgets are fun to use and most of them work, so don't hesitate to try them. Use the following finishing techniques to make pom-poms easier and professional looking.

Perfect Pom-Pom

Cut two cardboard circles ½" (1.3 cm) larger than the width of the desired pom-pom. Cut a ¾" (2-cm) hole in the center of each circle. Cut a small wedge of each circle away to make it easier to wrap the yarn. Place a tie strand between the two circles before wrapping. Wrap yarn around both circles many times. The more wraps, the thicker the pom-pom. Insert scissors between circles and carefully cut around outer edge to release yarn. Knot the tie strand tightly around center of yarn lengths. Gently ease cardboard from the pom-pom. Cut two cardboard circles the width of the desired pom-pom with pinpoint center holes. Place pom-pom between circles. Insert long weaving needle through pinpoint holes in cardboard and center of pom-pom. Trim around circles to even pom-pom.

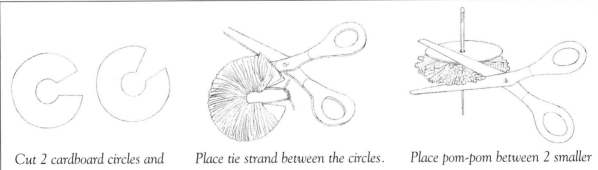

Cut 2 cardboard circles and cut a circle out of the center and a wedge out of the side of each.

Place tie strand between the circles. Wrap yarn around circles. Cut between circles and knot tie strand tightly.

Place pom-pom between 2 smaller cardboard circles held together with a needle, and trim the edges.

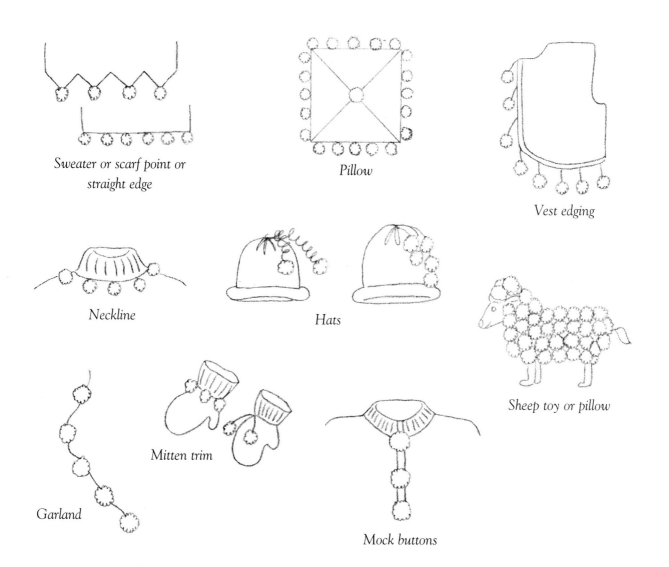

Sweater or scarf point or straight edge

Pillow

Vest edging

Neckline

Hats

Sheep toy or pillow

Garland

Mitten trim

Mock buttons

Pom-poms can be used on just about anything.

Ties

The following are the most common knitted ties used for pom-poms and tassels. Choose a tie that works well with the yarns you've used for your tassels or pom-poms.

Two-Color Finger-Cord

Cut 1 length each of 2 colors approximately 3 times the desired finished length of the tie. Tie the 2 yarns tog with an overhand knot. Make a loop with the light yarn around a loop of the dark yarn. Place your left index finger through the dark loop and hold the knot with your left thumb and middle finger. Tighten the light yarn by pulling it close to the knot. *Insert your right index finger into the front of the loop held by your left finger, hook it under the light yarn, and draw a light loop through. Remove your left finger and tighten the dark yarn by pulling it close to the knot. Working with your left index finger, draw a loop of dark yarn through the light loop and tighten in the same way. Repeat from * for desired length.

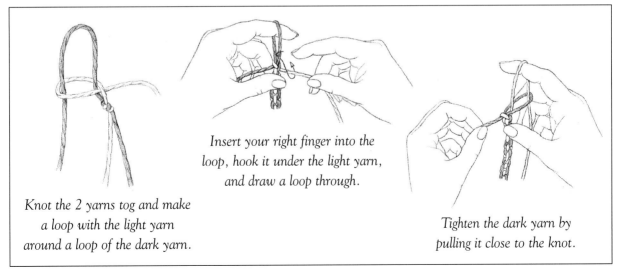

Knot the 2 yarns tog and make a loop with the light yarn around a loop of the dark yarn.

Insert your right finger into the loop, hook it under the light yarn, and draw a loop through.

Tighten the dark yarn by pulling it close to the knot.

Crochet Chain

Work crochet chain for desired length. Fasten off.

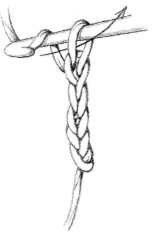

Knit Tie

CO number of sts for desired length. BO.

Three-Color Braid

Work a simple braid on 3 lengths of yarn, each a different color.

Two-Color Braid

Work 4-strand braid on 4 lengths of yarn, 2 each of 2 colors.

Creative Combinations

The following pieces I designed over the years for publication in a variety of knitting magazines. Keeping in mind the editorial themes outlined by the editors, I draw much of my inspiration from nature.

In designing, I give serious consideration to garment shape, stitch pattern, yarn type, and most of all, unique detail. All these pieces feature at least one technique I've outlined in the previous five chapters.

Drawing from whatever inspires you, I hope these examples will serve as a springboard for your own design and embellishment ideas. They should help you add your own personal touches and take satisfaction in creating one-of-a-kind handknits.

Child's Patchwork Hat

This colorwork hat is edged with multicolored garter-stitch scallops overlaid on a garter-stitch border. Corkscrew tassels give the hat a playful look.

Point Floral Pullover

This wool stockinette-stitch sweater features a deeply pointed front and a vertical rib border. It is embellished with fly stitch, decadent daisy stitch, French knots, stemmed French knots, fishbone stitch, straight stitch, and couching with cross-stitch, all worked in wool.

Floral Peplum Cardigan

A cabled peplum enhances the feminity of this alpaca sweater. Other features include a ruffle-stitch neckband and embroidered double-daisy stitch, French knots, stem stitch, and straight stitch worked in wool and metallic yarns.

Berry Time Pullover

Cables rise out of the edgings to define reverse stockinette-stitch panels that are enhanced with embroidery. Stem stitches and clusters of French knots (worked in two colors) are repeated throughout in an allover design.

Sampler Pullover

Modeled after an antique sampler, this wool sweater features cross-stitch worked with a few plies of tapestry wool. The traditional motifs include the alphabet, numbers, a schoolhouse, and various borders.

Two-Tone Cardigan

Worked in a silk/wool yarn, this sweater features a rib and cable pattern. Note that the ribbing on the sleeves works into the cable pattern without interruption, and that the collar is edged with the same ribbing. Elongated North stars embroidered with a slightly contrasting color accentuate the diamond shapes.

Wolf in Sheep's Clothing Sweater

This child's sweater is one in a series I designed that features Aesop's fables. In addition to traditional ribbing, the lower edges of the body and sleeves have colorwork borders. To give the sheep's coat more realistic dimension, I worked it in a bouclé yarn. Duplicate stitch, straight stitch, and French knots add detail and interest.

Angora Peplum Sweater

Bouquets of daisy stitches worked in silk ribbon and punctuated with pearl beads add to the elegance of this white-on-white angora sweater. Although the flowers would be pretty in colored yarn, I chose to work them in white to give the sweater a more sophisticated look.

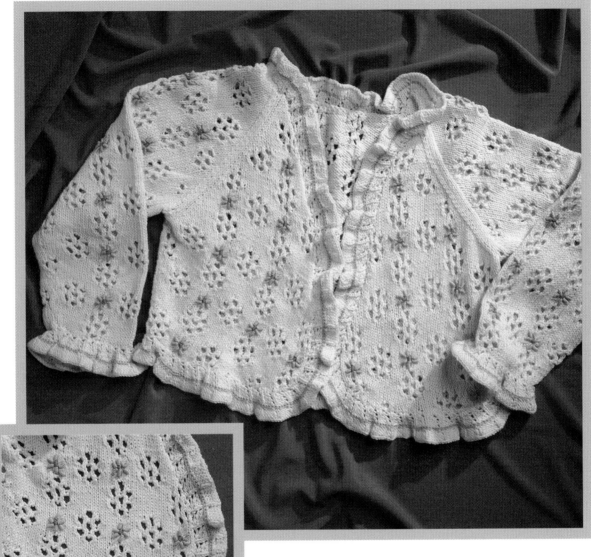

Ruffle Stitch Bolero

This cotton bolero is worked in an allover pawprint eyelet stitch and edged with ruffle stitch. Contrasting embroidered bouillon-stitch flowers and a simple chain-stitch detail add interest to the piece.

Farmscape Pullover

This farm scene is worked in intarsia and the small color details are added with duplicate stitch. Embroidered straight stitches with French-knot centers form the small flowers; daisy and stem stitches worked around single duplicate stitches form the sunflowers.

Grape Pillow

Worked in reverse stockinette stitch, this pillow is decorated with appliquéd leaves, embroidered stem stitch, and individual bobbles arranged in clusters.

Bib Lace Collar

This collar is knitted in an allover diamond lace stitch and edged with knit cord. The flowers and leaves are worked separately and sewn in place. Pearl beads add texture and grace.

Angel Sweater

This sweater combines a rather ordinary shape with a distinctive color-block border, intarsia angel motifs, double cross-stitch stars, and pattern stitch. Notice how the colors in the border pick up those in the intarsia motifs and how the pattern stitch mimics the shape of the embroidered stars.

Lace and Floral Cardigan

Vine-lace edges and collar border an otherwise simple sweater decorated with duplicate-stitch flowers and leaves. The collar lace is worked separately, gathered, and sewn in place, adding grace to the "hanging" floral motifs.

Fruit Still-Life Pullover

The vine-lace borders on this sweater give the impression that the intarsia still life sits on a lace tablecloth. Details in the still life are embroidered stem stitch, duplicate stitch, and running stitch.

Log Cabin Patchwork Pullover

This sweater combines many of the techniques outlined in this book. It is worked in individual patches of intarsia or solid colors adorned with appliqué and embroidery. The large patch featuring a log cabin and appliqué trees is the main focus, while a double border of garter stitch and multicolor points frames the lower edges and neckline, and brings continuity to the piece.

Glossary

Cast-Ons

Cable Cast-On: Cast on two stitches. Insert the right needle between the two stitches on the left needle (1). Wrap the yarn as if to knit. Draw the yarn through to complete the stitch (2), and slip the new stitch onto the left needle (3).

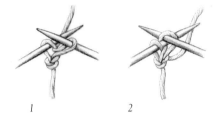

Knitted Cast-On: Make a slip knot and place it on a needle held in your left hand. *With a free needle, knit into the slip knot (1) and place the new st twisted onto the left needle (2)—2 sts on left needle

Repeat from *, always knitting into the last st made (not the slip knot).

Provisional Cast-On: Leaving tails about 4" (10 cm) long, tie a length of waste yarn together with the main yarn in an overhand knot. With your right hand, hold the knot on top of the needle a short distance from the tip, then place your thumb and index finger between the two yarns and hold the long ends with your other fingers. Hold your hand with your palm facing upwards and spread your thumb and index finger apart so that the yarn forms a V with the main yarn over your index finger and the waste yarn over your thumb. Bring the

needle up through the waste-yarn loop on your thumb from front to back. Place the needle over the main yarn on your index finger, and then back through the loop on your thumb. Drop the loop off your thumb and, placing your thumb back in the V configuration, tighten up the stitch on the needle. Repeat for the desired number of stitches. The main yarn will form the stitches on the needle and the waste yarn will make the horizontal ridge at the base of the cast-on row.

When it's time to pick up the cast-on stitches, carefully cut and pull out the waste yarn as you place the exposed loops on a needle. Take care to pick up the loops so that they are in the proper orientation before you begin knitting.

Glossary

Invisible Cast-On: Make a slip knot (A) and place it on the left needle. Pull the waste yarn from left to right through the loop and lay it underneath the needle. Hold the slip knot and waste yarn in place with your left hand. Wind the main yarn around the needle and the waste yarn over and away from you, under

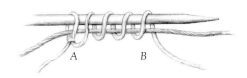

and towards you. As you get near end B, pull a little more waste yarn through. Make as many turns as you need stitches. Simply pull the waste yarn out when you are ready to pick up and work the loops along the cast-on edge.

Backward Loop Cast-On: Make a loop in the yarn and place it on the needle backward so that it doesn't unwind. Repeat for desired number of stitches, adjusting tension as needed.

Increases

M1 Increase: With left needle tip, lift the strand between the last knitted stitch and the first stitch on the left needle from front to back and place on left needle (1). Knit the lifted strand through the back loop (2).

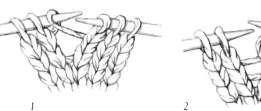

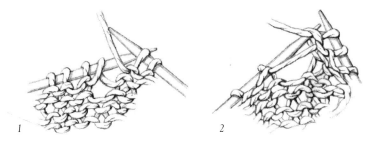

M1 Pwise Increase: With left needle tip, lift the strand between the last knitted stitch and the first stitch on the left needle, from back to front and place on left needle (1). Purl the lifted loop (2).

Decreases

Ssk Decrease: Slip two stitches knitwise, one at a time, to right needle (1). Insert the point of the left needle into the front of the two slipped stitches and knit them together through the back loop with the right needle (2).

1

2

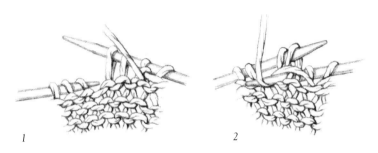

1   2

Ssp Decrease: Holding the yarn in front, slip two stitches (one at a time) knitwise onto the right needle (1). Slip them back onto left needle and purl the two stitches together through back loops (2).

Kitchener stitch

1. Bring threaded needle through the front stitch as if to purl and leave the stitch on the needle.

2. Bring threaded needle through the back stitch as if to knit and leave the stitch on the needle.

3. Bring threaded needle through the same front stitch as if to knit and slip this stitch off the needle. Bring the threaded needle through the next front stitch as if to purl and leave the stitch on the needle.

4. Bring threaded needle through the first back stitch as if to purl, slip that stitch off, and then bring the needle through the next back stitch as if to knit, and leave this stitch on the needle.

Repeat Steps 3 and 4 until no stitches remain

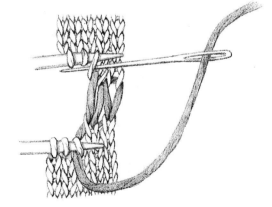

Crochet chain

Make a slipknot and place on a crochet hook. Yarn over the hook and draw it through the loop on the hook. Repeat, drawing the yarn through the last loop formed.

Knitting with Beads

Any size bead or yarn can be used for this technique as long as the holes of the beads are large enough to slide onto the yarn without damaging it. Start with the beads strung on the knitting yarn. Ideally, all the beads will be prestrung, but if you're working on a large piece with many beads it may be necessary to string the beads in sections. Knitting with too many prestrung beads is cumbersome because you have to continually slide the beads down the yarn to free enough yarn to knit with.

Stringing Beads: To transfer prestrung beads onto knitting yarn, simply tie the thread the beads come on to the knitting yarn and slide the beads from one to the other. Make the first half of an overhand knot, forming a loop, in the thread holding the beads. "Thread" this loop with the yarn and tighten the loop into a knot. Then carefully slide the beads over this knot and onto the yarn.

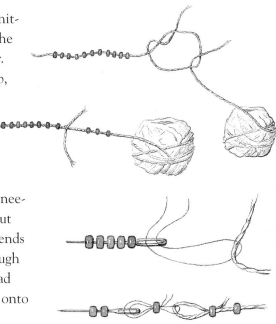

To string loose beads, use a beading needle. If your thread is too thick to go through the eye of the needle, use an intermediary thread. Take a length of fine but strong thread and fold it in half. Thread the two loose ends through the needle, then thread the knitting yarn through the loop of the intermediary thread. Now you can thread beads onto the needle, to the intermediary thread, and onto the knitting thread.

Beaded Knitting: This technique places the designated number of beads between two stitches. This means that the beads show on the back of the work. When bead(s) lie between two purl stitches, they show on the front of the work.

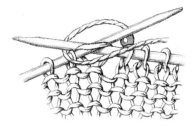

Work the stitch, slide up the designated number of beads right next to the stitch just worked (designated as SB1 for 1 bead), and work the next stitch.

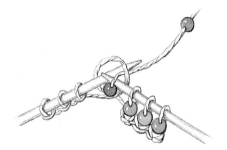

Bead Knitting: Use this technique to knit (or purl) a bead into a stitch. It is designated as BK1 for knitting, BP1 for purling.

Insert the needle into the stitch to be knit (or purled) as usual, slide a bead up against the needle, and pull the bead through to the front as you complete the stitch.

Felting

You can felt anything made of pure wool. Most of the appliques in this chapter lend themselves beautifully to felting. For consistency, felt all the pieces for a project at the same time. Note that felting will cause the pieces to shrink by about a third.

*Place the pieces to be felted into a sink filled with hot water and detergent. Use your hands to agitate them. Transfer the pieces to a basin of icy cold water and agitate again. Repeat from * until the wool has matted. Squeeze out excess water and allow the pieces to air dry.

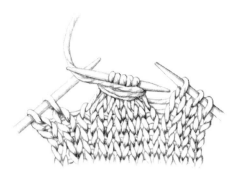

Wrap Stitches

Place specified number of (worked or unworked) stitches onto a cable needle. Wrap the working yarn around these stitches in the specified direction (clockwise shown) for the specified number of times. Place the stitches onto the right needle and continue row.

Two-Color Finger-Knit Cord

1. Tie the two colors of yarn together in an overhand knot. Make a loop with the light yarn around a loop of the dark yarn. Place your left finger through the dark loop and hold the knot with your left thumb and middle finger. Pull the light yarn with your right hand to tighten the light loop close to the knot.

2. Insert your right index finger into the front of the loop held by your left finger, hook it under the light yarn held in your right hand, and draw the loop through.

3. Remove your left finger and pull on the dark yarn to tighten the dark loop close to the knot.

4. In the same manner, insert your left index finger into the front of the light loop held by your right finger, hook it under the dark yarn held in your left hand, and draw the loop through. Remove your right finger and pull on the light yarn to tighten the light loop close to the knot.

Repeat Steps 2–4 for desired length.

Two-Color Plaited Tie

Knot four strands (two light, two dark, and each 1½ times the desired finished length) in an overhand knot at one end. Hook or pin this end to secure it. Position the strands so that the light strands are on the outside and the dark ones on the inside. Working from the outside, take the left strand over its nearest center strand, and the right strand over its nearest center strand as well as the strand just placed in the center. Continue placing the strands in the center, alternating sides so that like-colored strands form a V shape.

Applied Fringe

Cut several strands of yarn (the more strands, the thicker the fringe) two times the desired fringe length, plus about 1" (2.5 cm) for knotting. Fold the yarn in half. Insert a crochet hook into the knitted piece from back to front, catch the folded yarn, and pull it through the knitting. Draw the yarn ends through the loop and pull to tighten. Trim ends to even lengths.

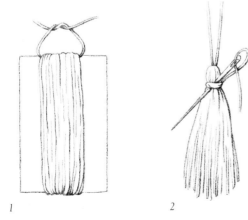

1

2

Tassel

Cut a piece of stiff cardboard the desired tassel length. Loop yarn around the cardboard the desired number of times (the more times, the fatter the tassel). Tie one end of the loops with a piece of tie yarn (1). Slip the loops off the cardboard and tie another piece of yarn around the loops near the top (2). Cut the ends of the loops and trim, if desired.

Glossary

Perfect Pom-Pom

1. Cut two cardboard circles ½" (1.3 cm) larger in diameter than the desired finished size. Cut a ¾" (2-cm) hole in the center of each circle. Cut away a small wedge of each circle to make it easier to wrap the yarn. Place a tie strand of yarn between the circles and hold them together, with both openings together. Wrap yarn around the circles the desired number of times (the more wraps, the thicker the pom-pom).

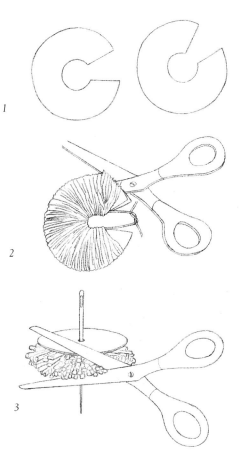

2. Insert scissors between circles and carefully cut around the outer edge to release the yarn. Knot the tie strand tightly around the group of yarn. Gently ease the cardboard from the pom-pom.

3. Cut two cardboard circles ½" (1.3 cm) smaller than the first two (the diameter of the desired finished size). Poke a pinpoint hole in the center of each circle. Sandwich the pom-pom between these two circles and insert a long tapestry needle through the hole in one circle, though the center of the pompom and out through the hole in the other circle. This will hold the pom-pom in place as you trim around the edges of the circles to even out the pom-pom.

Twisted Cord

Cut several lengths of yarn 4 to 5 times the desired finished cord length. Fold the strands in half, forming two groups. Anchor the strands at the fold.

1. Holding a group in each hand, twist each group tightly clockwise until it kinks.

2. Put both groups in one hand, then release them, allowing them to twist around each other counterclockwise. Secure the end with an overhand knot.

Abbreviations

1/1RC	1/1 right cross: place 1 st onto cn and hold in front, k1, k1 on cn	dpn(s)	double pointed needle(s)
1/1LC	1/1 left cross: place 1 st onto cn and hold in front, k1, k1 on cn	k	knit
		k1f&b	knit in front and back of stitch
1/1RCP	1/1 right cross purl: place 1 st onto cn and hold in back, k1, p1 on cn	inc('d)	increase(d); increasing
		k1b	knit through the back loop
1/1LCP	1/1 left cross purl: place 1 st onto cn and hold in front, p1, k1 on cn	k2tog	knit 2 stitches together
		kwise	knitwise
2/2RC	2/2 right cross: place 2 sts onto cn and hold in back, k2, k2 on cn	LT	left twist: sl 2 sts individually to right needle kwise, sl back to left needle, k2tog tbl, then knit first st again
2/2LC	2/2 left cross: place 2 sts onto cn and hold in front, k2, k2 on cn		
2/3LCP	2/3 left cross purl: place 2 sts onto cn and hold in front, p3, k2 sts on cn	m	marker
		MB	make bobble: see specific pattern for instructions
2/3RCP	2/3 right cross purl: place 3 sts onto cn and hold in back, k2, p3 on cn	MC	main color
		meas	measures
3/1RCP	3/1 right cross purl: place 1 st onto cn and hold in back, k3, p1 on cn	M1	make 1: increase by lifting running thread between stitch just made and next stitch from front to back, and knitting the lifted strand through back loop
3/1LCP	3/1 left right cross purl: place 3 sts onto cn and hold in front, p1, k3 on cn		
3/3RC	3/3 right cross: place 3 sts onto cn and hold in back, k3, k3 on cn	M1 pwise	make 1 purlwise: increase by lifting running thread between stitch just made and next stitch from back to front, and purling the lifted loop
3/3LC	3/3 left cross: place 3 sts onto cn and hold in front, k3, k3 on cable		
beg	begin(ning)	mock cable	knit 3rd stitch on left needle, knit 1st stitch, then 2nd stitch; drop all stitches from needle
BO	bind off		
CC(2)	contrast color (2)	mult	multiple
ch	chain	p	purl
cn	cable needle	p1b	purl through back loop of stitch
CO	cast on	p1f&b	purl in front and back of stitch
cont	continue; continuing	psso	pass slipped stitch over
dec('d)	decrease(d); decreasing	p2sso	pass 2 slipped stitches over

p2tog	purl 2 stitches together	ssp	slip 2 stitches individually to right needle knitwise, slip left needle through front of stitches and p2tog
pm	place marker		
pwise	purlwise		
rem(s)	remain(s); remaining	tbl	through back loop
rep	repeat	st(s)	stitch(es)
RS	right side	St st	stockinette stitch
RT	right twist: knit second st on left needle, then knit first st.	T2	twist 2: knit next 2 stitches together, then knit first stitch again
SB1	slip 1, or designated number of, bead(s)	wyib	with yarn in back
		wyif	with yarn in front
sl	slip	WS	wrong side
ssk	slip 2 stitches individually to right needle knitwise, slip left needle through front of stitches and k2tog through back loop	yb	bring yarn to back of needles
		yf	bring yarn to front of needles
		yo	yarn over

Chart Symbols

b	k1 tbl	⅄	sl 1 kwise, k2tog, psso	•	purl on RS; knit on WS
e	backward loop cast on	⅄	sl 1 pwise, p2tog, psso	●	bobble
M	make 1	☐	knit on RS; purl on WS	↗	k3tog
⌄³	knit front, back, and front of same st	☐	pattern repeat	↘	p3tog
⌄²	knit front and back of same st	＼	ssk on RS; ssp on WS	∧	sl 2tog kwise, k1, p2sso
⌄⁰	k1, yo, k1 in same st	／	k2tog on RS; p2tog on WS	↙	p2tog
⌒	bind off	○	yo	↘	p2tog tbl
■	st left on needle after BO	ⱔ	sl 1 wyif	╱4	k4tog
	no stitch, unless otherwise noted	V	sl 1 wyib	⍓4	sl 4 sts individually kwise, insert left needle into fronts of these sts and knit them tog tbl

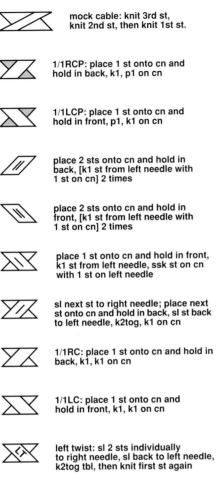

mock cable: knit 3rd st, knit 2nd st, then knit 1st st.

1/1RCP: place 1 st onto cn and hold in back, k1, p1 on cn

1/1LCP: place 1 st onto cn and hold in front, p1, k1 on cn

place 2 sts onto cn and hold in back, [k1 st from left needle with 1 st on cn] 2 times

place 2 sts onto cn and hold in front, [k1 st from left needle with 1 st on cn] 2 times

place 1 st onto cn and hold in front, k1 st from left needle, ssk st on cn with 1 st on left needle

sl next st to right needle; place next st onto cn and hold in back, sl st back to left needle, k2tog, k1 on cn

1/1RC: place 1 st onto cn and hold in back, k1, k1 on cn

1/1LC: place 1 st onto cn and hold in front, k1, k1 on cn

left twist: sl 2 sts individually to right needle, sl back to left needle, k2tog tbl, then knit first st again

right twist: knit 2nd st on left needle, then knit first st

2/2RC: place 2 sts onto cn and hold in back, k2, k2 on cn

2/2LC: place 2 sts onto cn and hold in front, k2, k2 on cn

place 2 sts onto cn and hold in front, k2, k1 on cn, ssk last st on cn with p1st

sl next st (p1) to right needle, place next 2 sts onto cn and hold in back, sl purl st back to left needle, k2tog (first knit st and purl st), k1, k2 on cn

3/3RC: place 3 sts onto cn and hold in back, k3, k3 on cn

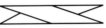
3/3LC: place 3 sts onto cn and hold in front, k3, k3 on cn

3/1RCP: place 1 st onto cn and hold in back, k3, p1 on cn

3/1LCP: place 3 sts onto cn and hold in front, p1, k3 on cn

2/3LCP: place 2 sts onto cn and hold in front; p3, k2 on cn

2/3 RCP: place 3 sts onto cn and hold in back, k2, p3 on cn

Index

Index